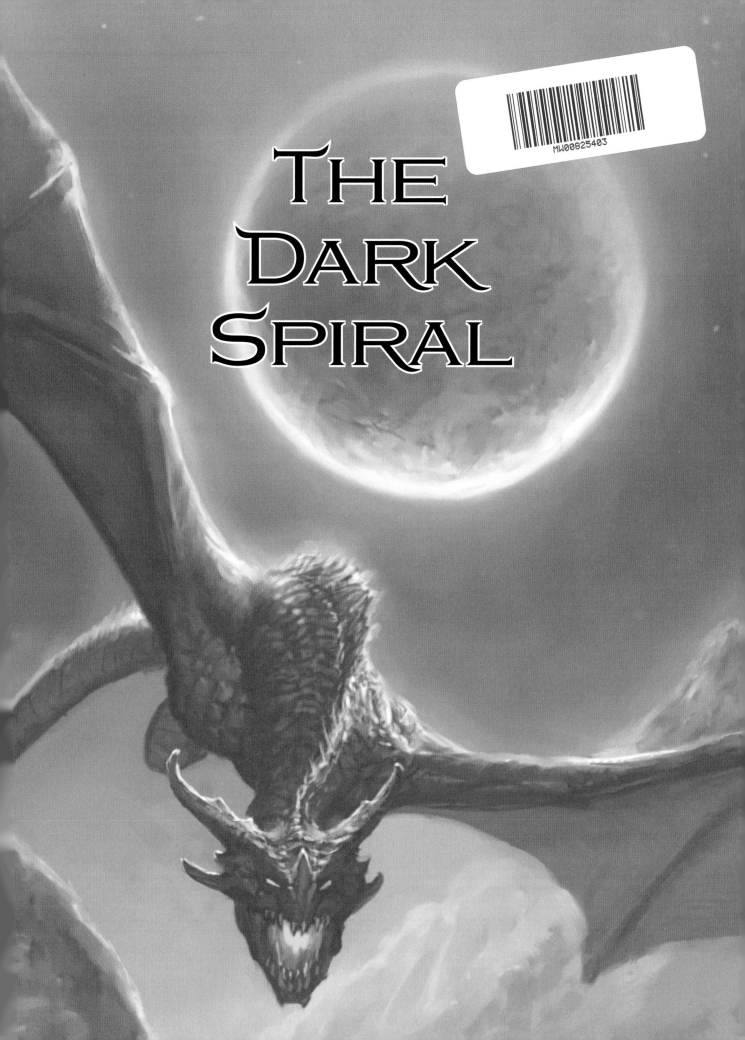

THE DARK SPIRAL

Credits

Writer/Designer
Bruce R. Cordell

Lead Editor
Shanna Germain

Editor and Proofreader
Ray Vallese

Cover Artist
Matt Stawicki

Graphic Designer
Sarah Robinson

Artists
Nicholas Cloister, Jason Engle, Erebus, Eric Lofgren, Patrick McEvoy, Grzegorz Pedrycz, Mike Perry, Michael Phillippi, Joe Slucher, Lee Smith, Matt Stawicki, Cyril Terpent, Tiffany Turrill, Cathy Wilkins

Cartographer Hugo Solis

Monte Cook Games Editorial Team
Scott C. Bourgeois, David Wilson Brown, Eric Coates, Gareth Hodges, Ryan Klemm, Jeremy Land, Laura Wilkinson, George Ziets

Special Thanks
Torah Cottrill

Printed in Canada

TABLE OF CONTENTS

INTRODUCTION

The Dark Spiral *provides player characters (PCs) with several opportunities for side adventures while they pursue the main arc. In addition, the major sections of the book can be played as part of that main plot arc, making* The Dark Spiral *a mini-campaign, or as separate adventures presented in whole or in part by you, the game master (GM). However, some chapters of the main arc follow more naturally from earlier chapters than others do, so that's the order presented here. Obviously, the material in this product is for the GM only.*

COREBOOK CALLOUTS
Throughout this adventure, you'll see page references to various items accompanied by this symbol. These are page references to The Strange *corebook, where you can find additional details about that item, place, rule, NPC, or creature. It isn't usually necessary to look up the referenced items in the corebook; it's an optional way to learn more about the situation and provide additional information to your players. The exception is if a cypher or creature stat is referenced, in which case you'll want the corebook nearby.*

CHARACTERS

This adventure works well with beginning characters. More advanced characters might require the GM to make a few modifications (suggestions are provided when appropriate). The action starts on the campus of a covert private agency called the Estate, so running the adventure requires the least adaptation if the PCs are operatives or associates of that organization. Either way, it's best if most of the PCs know one another ahead of time; the connection information in the characters' descriptors should be enough to join them together. The most obvious initial hooks to get characters involved assume that they're available to be assigned new missions by the Estate. If this isn't the case, use one of the alternative ideas for involving your PCs.

OVERVIEW

The first section of the book, "Estate Home Base," presents the PCs with a convenient and useful hub. In addition to providing hooks and a framing narrative, "Estate Home Base" also presents several adventures. You can use one of them to introduce the PCs to the main story of *The Dark Spiral*. That arc could unfold as follows.

ESTATE HOME BASE

The PCs are fresh Estate operatives with few (if any) successful missions under their belt. Among several minor missions the characters might be assigned to investigate is one that connects directly to the main arc of *The Dark Spiral*: stop a drug dealer who sells spiral dust. Although that mission seems fairly straightforward, the Estate rewards initial success by asking the PCs to roll up the entire spiral dust operation, which requires far more investment by the characters.

Seeking after clues that will lead to the source of the spiral dust, the PCs eventually discover leads implicating a shop in the mountain town of Nederland, Colorado.

While other missions are ongoing, the PCs have the opportunity to return to the Estate campus. There they can rest, request material aid, research newly discovered aspects of their current mission, and so on. In addition to player-instigated events, two other events happen while the PCs are at the base.

INTERMISSION 1

The campus is attacked by... zombies? During or after the attack, it's determined that the "zombies" are actually spiral dust-maddened people whose addiction to the drug somehow triggered an awful transformation.

INTERMISSION 2

The PCs meet an Estate consultant, an entity of the Strange called Uentaru, who shares the organization's concern about ending the spiral dust drug trade. The PCs are asked to share their intelligence and resources, and work with Uentaru to accomplish their goal.

NEVER, NEDERLAND

The spiral dust distribution center in Nederland, Colorado, is the Dreaming Crystal rock shop. The shop can be infiltrated and shut down. In doing so, the PCs discover that the site receives its spiral dust supply from another recursion—apparently, directly through a crime family head in a recursion called Crow Hollow.

A Beak Mafia crime boss known as Donna Ilsa finds the spiral dust trade profitable, but lately intrafamily squabbles have taken center stage. She is willing to work with Estate operatives and roll over on her supplier, but in return, she requests a gift. Her eggs were kidnapped and are being held in Ardeyn. She asks the PCs to return them to her. If the PCs succeed in returning her eggs from a location

called the Mouth of Swords, they gain Donna Ilsa's cooperation. She gives them plans to a location in Ruk where the spiral dust is processed.

MOUTH OF SWORDS

The Mouth of Swords occasionally attracts Ardeyn adventurers, given the place's reputation as a depository of valuables and magical treasures. PCs who venture to the site are in for a "classic" adventure featuring exploration, puzzles, and fearsome creatures of Ardeyn. Once the PCs retrieve some or all of Donna Ilsa's eggs, she gives them what they need to find and enter the spiral dust lab in Ruk.

WHOLE BODY GRAFTS

To gain access to the spiral dust production facility in Ruk, the characters must infiltrate or battle their way past venom troopers and other guardians of a business called Whole Body Grafts. Upon doing so, they discover that the drug lab is a "place" all its own called Nakarand.

The lord of Nakarand is the Dustman, a sort of nightmarish sandman and the ultimate supplier of spiral dust. The PCs learn that the Dustman's method of generating spiral dust is nothing less than ghoulish. From

captives inside Nakarand, or possibly from the Dustman himself, the PCs learn that Uentaru helped the Dustman distribute spiral dust across Earth. She is not there to help the PCs but to make sure they don't succeed. Why? Because spiral dust causes its users to enter a state similar to being quickened, and having more quickened people on Earth will empower the Aleph component hidden in the planet's crust. The Aleph component could be used to recreate Uentaru's vanished homeworld, despite the fact that doing so would likely destroy the Earth and all the recursions around it.

JOURNEY TO THE CENTER OF THE EARTH

To find the Aleph component, switch it off, and save the planet, the characters must travel under the Earth's mantle, perhaps using a special recursion engine vehicle (REV) created by the Estate's Research Chief Hertzfeld. Penetrating the mantle is difficult enough. But surviving the environment, defeating the horrifying guardian that Uentaru left behind, and possibly having to choose between their own lives and the continued existence of planet Earth will push the PCs to their limit, and perhaps beyond.

SHOW 'EM ILLUSTRATIONS
Throughout this adventure, you'll also see the symbol above. This denotes that the image on the page is a Show 'Em. These images are designed to be shown to your players when they come upon a particular scene in the adventure. The symbols are accompanied by a page number as well as a Show 'Em letter. Show 'Ems are found toward the back of the book, starting on page 91.

ESTATE HOME BASE

This section of the book provides the PCs with a hub where other adventures are assigned and where they can rest and restock provisions between missions. In addition to providing hooks for the other adventure sections in the book, "Estate Home Base" has its own adventure content (beginning with "Spiral Dust Drug Bust" on page 16), which you can use separately or as part of the main plot arc.

The Estate, page 148

BACKGROUND

To the world at large, the Estate is a philanthropic institute that funds research in several scientific fields of inquiry. While that's partly true (the facade works because the group *does* award scientific grants to deserving causes on a yearly basis), the Estate is actually a secret organization that actively but covertly protects the Earth from all threats from the Strange.

SYNOPSIS

Whether as operatives of the Estate or through other connections, the PCs can take part in several minor missions. These missions (including two intermissions) are described in this chapter. The PCs also have the opportunity to interact more fully with the Estate staff and facility. When you decide the time is right, the PCs receive the assignment that begins the main arc: putting an end to local drug dealer LeRoy Cain.

NPC guard, page 303

NPC agent, page 302

Estate roster, page 149

NOT AN ESTATE OPERATIVE?

The default assumption in *The Dark Spiral* is that PCs are already members of the Estate. If you're not using that assumption, getting the PCs involved in the minor missions and the main arc merely requires a little more work on your part. To help you, each minor mission, each intermission, and the main adventure arc contains at least one idea for involving non-Estate PCs.

MINOR MISSIONS

Most minor missions are short and self-contained, though they could serve as hooks to longer play if you desire. You can use some,

Assigning one or more SOs to the PCs is great for a group that enjoys roleplaying. Each potential SO described has a strong personality that the GM can use to make the PCs' lives easier, harder, or, at the very least, a lot more interesting.

● ○ ○
ESTATE SECURITY PROCEDURES

• Locks, individual alarm systems, encrypted Wi-Fi, and related elements are level 6.

• All buildings on the Estate campus remain locked at all times, usually requiring someone from the outside to get through two to four locked checkpoints to reach a secure objective. Each operative is issued a personalized ten-digit code to gain access to areas he has clearance for.

• An individual alarm system is wired into each building. Accessing a building's alarm is a difficulty 7 Intellect task, and accessing the entire Estate security system at once is a difficulty 8 Intellect task.

• CCTV cameras are installed at strategic points around the Estate and are monitored by a rotating staff of level 4 NPC guards in the security building.

• At any one time, a detail of five security guards is on active duty patrolling the campus, with as many as twenty-five more guards on call. Up to four NPC agents and four principal members of the Estate roster might also be on site at any given time to help during a security emergency.

● ○ ○

all, or none of these minor missions, in any order, or as PC interest dictates.

SUPERVISING OFFICER ASSIGNMENT

The Estate follows some (but not all) of the procedures of a secret government agency. One of the policies the group sometimes chooses to invoke is that of assigning a supervising officer (SO) to new operatives. If the PCs are lucky enough to get one, they might be assigned one SO for the whole group, or different SOs might be assigned to

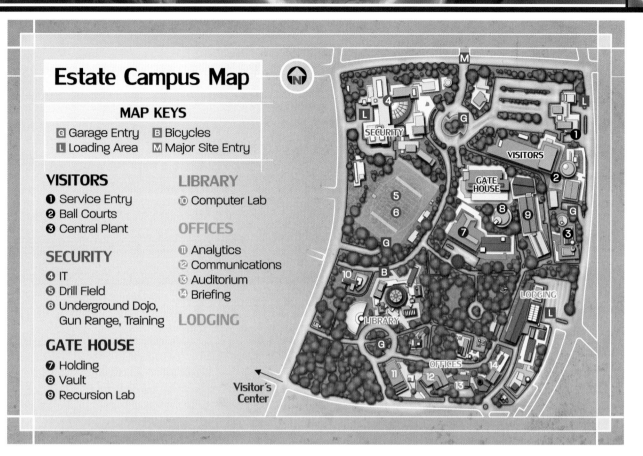

Estate Campus Map

MAP KEYS

G Garage Entry   B Bicycles
L Loading Area   M Major Site Entry

VISITORS
❶ Service Entry
❷ Ball Courts
❸ Central Plant

SECURITY
❹ IT
❺ Drill Field
❻ Underground Dojo,
   Gun Range, Training

GATE HOUSE
❼ Holding
❽ Vault
❾ Recursion Lab

LIBRARY
❿ Computer Lab

OFFICES
⓫ Analytics
⓬ Communications
⓭ Auditorium
⓮ Briefing

LODGING

Visitor's Center

different characters. Regardless, the PCs can accept other minor missions from this section as part of their training.

Non-Estate PCs: Being assigned a supervising officer requires the PCs to be members of the Estate. However, all the SO graduation tests described here provide hooks that can be used as separate mini-adventures for PCs who are not members of the organization.

SUPERVISING OFFICER KATHERINE J. MANNERS
Katherine Manners was a private detective and computer security consultant before she became the Estate's lead operative. If the GM assigns her as the SO for one or more of the PCs, she asks that they show up twice a week for a one-hour seminar set to last six weeks.

Look and Personality: Katherine Manners ("Kate" to her friends, but to the PCs, she first introduces herself as Lead Operative Manners) has red hair that's normally tied back. She presents a calm and collected persona but can be quick with a smile, a humorous quip, or, on rare occasion, a strong obscenity. She's open-minded to new information but not gullible.

Seminars: PCs who attend Manners's

seminars learn various methods of gathering evidence under false pretenses, usually by posing as a real estate agent, groundskeeper, courier, or plant-watering service provider in a large office building. She shows the PCs the kinds of kits they can request from the Estate for specific jobs (for instance, the group has a number of generic coveralls that can be configured for a variety of fake service jobs, props that go with each job, and a business card printer for sealing the masquerade). A

Experience Point Awards: PCs who pass a supervising officer's graduation test earn 2 XP in addition to any other XP the GM might award for a related adventure.

Katherine J. Manners: level 6

Katherine J. Manners, page 149

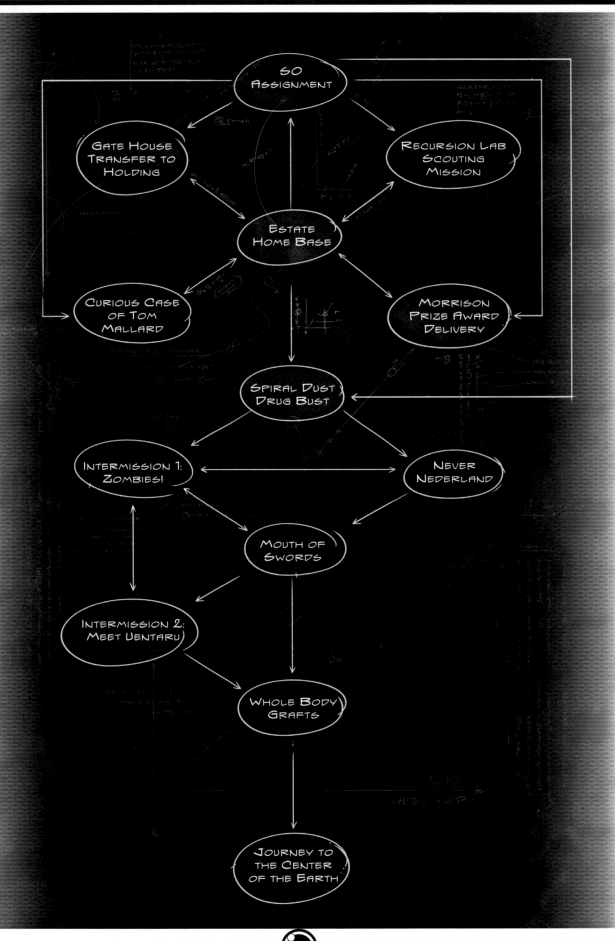

specifically requisitioned kit customized for the job at hand can serve as an asset during an intrusion attempt.

Graduation Test: Manners asks the PCs to see Liza Banks, the Estate's chief of public relations, and apply their newly acquired skills by posing as members of the Morrison Fellowship Prize delivery team. Before they leave, she gives each PC a randomly determined cypher (if they need one to reach their cypher limit).

SUPERVISING OFFICER LAWRENCE KEATON

Investigations Chief Lawrence Keaton was an insurance fraud investigator before coming to the Estate. If the GM assigns him as the SO for one or more of the PCs, he says he'll contact them later with details of the exercises he has planned.

Look and Personality: Lawrence Keaton is a thin man with unkempt hair. He is skeptical, obstinate, and, when encountered in his office, never without some sort of amber-colored liquid in a crystal glass. Despite how much alcohol he seems to drink, his diction is never slurred—quite the opposite, as if he's concentrating hard on pronouncing everything exactly right.

Exercises: Keaton mentions his exercises whenever he happens to see the PCs around the campus, indicating that he is working on them, it won't be long now, the characters are sure to learn a lot, and so on. However, even if they press Keaton, the exercises never materialize.

Graduation Test: Keaton contacts the PCs after a month and tells them they've been fast-tracked for graduation, and all they need to do is succeed on a simple internal security procedure. He assigns the PCs the task described under "Gate House Transfer to Holding" as their graduation test. Before they leave, he gives each PC a randomly determined cypher (if they need one to reach their cypher limit).

SUPERVISING OFFICER HERTZFELD

Research Chief Hertzfeld looks Caucasian, but he speaks with a Japanese accent. If the GM assigns him as the SO for one or more of the PCs, he asks them to show up at the drill ground once a week for four weeks for a training course that he developed for recursors.

Hertzfeld won't volunteer it, but if asked, he confirms that he is native to a recursion, not Earth. Other than that, he is not forthcoming (though if the PCs are so bold and skilled as to access his files, they learn that Hertzfeld takes a yearly three-week sabbatical to return to his recursion of origin—possibly one called Atom Nocturne, though that's not certain—where he tends something called the "Orchid").

Look and Personality: Hertzfeld's shock of blond hair seems untamable, and his glasses are more like goggles. He is rarely without his lab coat and a digital readout of some kind, which he obsessively checks even during other conversations. With so many experiments running concurrently, it's easy for him to fall behind on data collection.

Training Course: Each week for one hour, Hertzfeld ushers the PCs away from the drill field and into a rental van, then takes them on a tour of the following sites, one site per trip: the Seattle Aquarium (fish and other creatures of the sea), the Seattle Underground (what used to be street level for the city before it was built over), the Troll Under the Bridge in the Fremont neighborhood (a big cement troll under a bridge), and a tour of chocolatiers in the area. On each tour, Hertzfeld provides a running commentary of little-known facts pertinent to each location. He tries to be engaging, and it's obvious that he is quite excited by the tours. It may dawn on the characters that he uses the training to widen his own horizons. He obviously bones up with remarkable diligence before each trip, and PCs who pay attention can't help but learn things they never knew before.

Graduation Test: Hertzfeld explains one of his latest research projects to the characters: something called the REV. Their aid in resolving one of his outstanding research questions will serve as their graduation test. See "Recursion Lab Scouting Mission" for the full details. Before the PCs enter the odd recursion, he gives each character a randomly determined cypher (if they need one to reach their cypher limit).

MORRISON FELLOWSHIP PRIZE DELIVERY

Chief of Public Relations Liza Banks is responsible for putting together representatives of the Estate who hand out Morrison Fellowship Prizes to people working in any field who "demonstrate remarkable talent and the promise for continued creative

GMs can use the cypher list on page 312 of The Strange *corebook to provide randomly determined cyphers to players.*

Lawrence Keaton: level 6

Lawrence Keaton, page 149

Gate House Transfer to Holding, page 11

Recursion Lab Scouting Mission, page 12

Hertzfeld: level 5, level 7 for tasks related to scientific research

Hertzfeld, page 149

Morrison Fellowship Prize, page 148

work." However, the real reason the Estate gives out these prizes is so they can keep tabs on technical advances that might be due to effects of the Strange.

Liza tells one or more PCs that they've been selected to accompany her on a mission to Faribault, Minnesota, to award a prize to one Gwendolyn Wertz for her winning entry in the state science fair: how the heat of the human body can be used to power smartphones and other household objects. The Estate wants to make sure that Wertz or her advisor hasn't stumbled onto some sort of cypher or artifact from a recursion.

Non-Estate PCs: Gwendolyn Wertz blows away the Faribault science fair judges by producing a flashlight powered only by the touch of a human hand. Gwen's mom, Joyce, is on hand with a smile that almost seems brighter than the flashlight. She invites all the participants to her home for cake and ice cream to celebrate everyone's hard work. (The Joyce the PCs meet is actually an android called Joyce2.)

Weeks later, those children begin to disappear. Joyce2 is secretly stealing them and putting them in her basement to serve as additional batteries for a new project she has in mind: creating a recursion gate into the Strange. The PCs are asked to find out who's stealing Faribault children (or they choose to investigate on their own initiative).

Modifying for Higher Tiers: If the characters' average tier is 3 or 4, increase Joyce2's level by 3. If the PCs' average tier is 5 or 6, increase Joyce2's level by 5 and have her duplicate show up. See Modifying a Creature's Level for additional guidance.

Faribault, Minnesota: Faribault is the county seat for Rice County, Minnesota. It has a population of approximately 23,000 people and is about 50 miles south of Minneapolis. The Estate flies the PCs there in business class and puts them up in a hotel called the Regency Inn.

Liza Banks has a room in the same hotel. If needed, use NPC agent stats for Banks, except that she is level 7 in tasks related to persuasion.

Wertz Residence: Gwen lives with her mother, Joyce; her father, Tom, died a year ago in a traffic accident. The house seems normal enough, though all the lights are on at any given time. Joyce and Gwen knew the prize team would be coming and are overjoyed to welcome guests into their home, serving everyone doughnuts and pop (people in Minnesota call soda "pop").

Gwendolyn Wertz: level 2, level 8 for all tasks related to robotics and electronics

Modifying a Creature's Level, page 16

Liza Banks, page 149

Joyce2: level 5, level 6 for disguise tasks; health 28; Armor 3; inflicts 5 points of damage with two pummeling melee attacks per action

Gwen runs off to grab her Person Power Prototype One, which looks like a flashlight. If handled, bare skin contact causes the bulb to light. If a PC with an eye for the Strange examines the flashlight, it seems like nothing more than a particularly clever application of Standard Physics.

The prize delivery mission goes by the book—unless the facade crumbles.

The Facade Crumbles: If the PCs push Gwen or Joyce too hard on where the idea for the flashlight came from, what Gwen's next project will be, or some related topic, equanimity begins to fade. Gwen grows distressed but tries to hide it, while Joyce seems to show less and less emotion. Eventually, Gwen says, "Don't make Mommy angry!" to which Joyce (who's actually Joyce2) replies in a robotic monotone, "Too late."

If the PCs explore the house before, during, or after the confab with the family in the living room, they might find the *real* Joyce Wertz in the basement, strapped into a chair and connected to an artifact called the power rod. Her body powers the whole house. (The PCs can also find three anoetic cyphers in the basement on a work table filled with other equipment: a level 5 uninterruptible power source, a level 3 visual displacement device, and a level 5 set of wings.)

Joyce2 is an android that Gwen created to be her mom stand-in after her real mom become emotionally distant after the death of her husband. The creation of Joyce2 triggered Gwen's quickening, whereupon she gained strange abilities.

Unfortunately, Joyce2 took its new position a little too seriously. The android violently opposes any action that might lead to anyone discovering its true nature or trying to separate it from Gwen.

Repercussions: Gwendolyn Wertz, if she survives, could use psychological counseling, and her real mother (if rescued from the basement) could use a lot of medical care. If the PCs arrange for such treatment through the Estate, they are given a commendation. If they leave the task to Liza Banks, Gwen and Joyce still get help, but not as quickly or as fully, possibly leaving Gwen with permanent emotional damage, which she might one day decide to take out on the PCs.

Hertzfeld makes a good case for turning the power rod artifact over to him so he can conduct further tests on it. He is worried that

it might be too much of a strain on the laws of Standard Physics.

GATE HOUSE TRANSFER TO HOLDING

Investigations Chief Lawrence Keaton assigns one or more of the PCs to be on hand to provide additional security for a cross-recursion transfer, initiated by field operative Harper Nash. Operative Nash contacted the Estate via courier several days ago, letting the group know when she would be transferring a couple of green homunculi of Ardeyn through an inapposite gate exit in the Gate House, and from there remand the creatures to Holding (at the request of Hertzfeld, who wants to study them in a nontranslated state, before they begin to degrade).

The date and time of the transfer is today at 2:00 p.m.

Gate House: The Gate House contains permanent recursion gates (mostly translation gates, but a few inapposite gates) to various locations in Ardeyn, a few places in Ruk, and several lesser-known recursions. Most of these gates require some sort of key or password to use successfully, and each gate is secure within its own room, locked by keypad.

The Transfer: When the PCs show up to the designated gate at the indicated time (call it gate B4 on the B sublevel beneath the Gate House), the initial transfer goes well. Two

---

30 kWh is as much electricity as an average American home uses in one day, or about 100 miles (161 km) of travel for an electric car.

Show 'Em: The Transfer, Image A, page 91

Betrayer's homunculi, page 259

Ardeyn, page 160

Trick embedder, page 330

Ray emitter (mind-disrupting), page 326

NPC agent, page 302

NPC recursor, page 305

manacled green homunculi appear through the expected inapposite gate, accompanied by an agent wearing garb in the style of Ardeyn who identifies herself as Harper Nash. Also present is Lawrence Keaton, smelling noticeably of alcohol. He interacts with the PCs and with Nash, but he does not accompany anyone out of the Gate House. Rather, he goes his own way after telling Nash to take the subjects to Holding cell 208.

Though the homunculi came to Earth through an inapposite gate, their abilities do not begin degrading for a few minutes (as is normal for such travel), which is why Keaton asked the PCs to be on hand. The investigations chief may be in his cups, but he's no fool. And it's lucky the PCs are present because "agent" Harper Nash is actually a red homunculus in disguise (a disguise provided by a cypher, forging a facade that lasts for one hour and requires a successful difficulty 6 Intellect-based task to see through).

Escape Attempt: If the PCs become suspicious of Nash, or when the greens and "Nash" reach the 10-foot (3 m) wide, 40-foot (12 m) long underground corridor between the Gate House and Holding, the red and the two greens make a break for it. They launch a surprise attack at the PCs first because

they don't want anyone to know they've perpetrated a security breach.

Loot: The red homunculus posing as Nash carries two anoetic cyphers: a level 4 trick embedder and a level 7 ray emitter (mind-disrupting).

Repercussions: If the PCs defeat the homunculi, all well and good; the characters receive a commendation. If they have trouble, a security team consisting of three NPC agents and two NPC recursors shows up a minute after the conflict begins.

Non-Estate PCs: One of the PCs is friends with Harper Nash but doesn't know that she is an Estate operative. When she goes missing, the PCs arrive in her home, only to discover their "friend" Harper appearing through a gate with two green-skinned homunculi in tow.

Modifying for Higher Tiers: For each tier the characters' average tier is above 1, add two more green homunculi to the group being transferred. Even with modification, it's unlikely that high-tier characters will find this encounter challenging, though they might still find it interesting.

RECURSION LAB SCOUTING MISSION

Research Chief Hertzfeld has been testing the

creation of special custom recursions through various experimental methods as background research for his recursion engine vehicle (REV). He approaches the PCs and asks their help on a related matter.

• "I'm experimenting with recursion technology. I'm trying to emulate the quality Ruk once possessed that allowed it to travel the Chaosphere under the direction of a pilot. I've made a lot of progress.

• (Hertzfeld proudly shows the PCs the REV blueprint): "This craft, for instance, shows real promise. I call it the REV: the recursion engine vehicle. It's able to travel in normal space—not the dark energy network—by going out of phase with regular matter. I was hoping to use it as a way to eschew rocket engines for interplanetary travel, but it turns out that it's probably more immediately suited to traveling beneath the Earth's crust. Either way, I find the possibilities amazing."

• (Hertzfeld rolls up the blueprints): "But that's not your mission today—only background." (Hertzfeld is easily distracted with his many projects and enthusiasms.)

• "In developing the REV, I've also had a few setbacks. That's why I want your help. I've created gates into a few secondary recursions

that don't follow the expected rules. One in particular vexes me. I need someone to scout it and report back. The recursion is designated R639. I would love to take a team in myself, but I'm already too far behind on getting the REV up and running."

If the PCs are interested, Hertzfeld takes them to the Recursion Lab and shows them the gate to recursion R639.

Non-Estate PCs: One or more of the PCs receives an inheritance from a dead aunt: a rental storage unit containing strange odds and ends, plus a large mirror propped up against the rear wall. The mirror is the translation gate described below.

Modifying for Higher Tiers: If the optional encounter occurs, add one more thonik to the attacking swarm for each tier the characters' average tier is above 2. If the PCs are fifth- or sixth-tier characters, increase the level of the thoniks present by 2.

Recursion Lab: Research on the nature of gates, the interaction of laws, the nature of fundament, and related inquiry is conducted in this stand-alone structure. The lab usually contains about ten or fifteen technicians working at any one time. Several recursion gates are found here in locked cubbies, each

The recursion engine vehicle (REV) becomes important in the last chapter, "Journey to the Center of the Earth" (page 83).

Show 'Em: *REV, Image B, page 91*

flanked by scientific work benches filled with laboratory equipment.

Hertzfeld says the matter could be quickly resolved by sealing recursion R639, but it'd be a shame to close access to a location that might be rich in cyphers, artifacts, or newly discovered attributes.

R639, Mystery Recursion: The secondary recursion Hertzfeld wants the PCs to scout is codenamed R639. They can access it through an inapposite gate, which he has annealed to the surface of a large mirror that leans against the wall in a bare chamber accessible by keycode.

Hertzfeld and his technicians sent a robot through the gate (not unlike a bomb-disposal robot), which returned after spending some time on the other side taking pictures and measurements. That allowed them to determine that the recursion supports Standard Physics and looks almost exactly like Earth.

Entering R639: PCs who enter R639 discover a dim replica of the Estate campus, although one that seems to have been without power or people for several months. Cloud cover is constant and heavy, which means it's always dreary and cold. Beyond the campus, the rest of the city is also visible, equally dark and also without power.

A cursory examination would lead one to believe it really *is* the Earth (because no matter how far an explorer goes, the recursion seems to stretch farther), though an Earth where all higher animals, including humans, are missing.

If PCs explore further, they eventually find a disturbing aspect to R639. The basements and sublevels of the Estate and nearby structures are filled with empty clothes and desiccated dust. It's almost as if everyone retreated to the lowest place they could find but failed to escape whatever hunted them. Whatever found them left behind only a trace of ash and clothing. R639's previous population seems to have been utterly wiped out.

Cypher list, page 312

Thonik, page 294

● ○ ○

R639
Level: 4
Laws: Standard Physics, Exotic
Playable Races: None (translating in is impossible; the recursion can be accessed only by inapposite gate)
Foci: As Earth
Skills: As Earth
Connection to Strange: Above the clouds lies the Strange
Connection to Earth: One inapposite gate in the Estate's Recursion Lab
Size: Indeterminate
Spark: 0%
Trait: Afraid. The difficulty of all rolls to resist or fight off anxiety, fear, or panic is increased by one step.

● ○ ○

Loot: Despite being a "copy" of the campus in the real world, the Estate in R639 doesn't have the cyphers the real Estate possesses. That said, searching the "remains" yields 1d6 randomly determined cyphers.

Optional Encounter: PCs can get in and out of this foreboding recursion without learning what led to the current circumstances, but if they seem determined to find answers, you shouldn't disappoint them. In this case, their investigation finally uncovers something: a flock of *something strange* wings overhead. From a distance it's hard to tell what kind of birds they are, but when four of the flying things split off from the group, the PCs discover they're not birds at all, but something like sheets of fleshy clay shot through with undulating, mouthlike openings that appear, disappear, open, and close in rhythmic pulses.

The things attack the PCs and give no quarter. The flying sheets are thoniks.

This is a good time for the characters to make Intellect defense rolls to avoid a round of panic (see R639's trait). PCs who fail spend their next turn running scared, standing frozen in horror, fainting, or screaming their fool heads off (their choice). Affected characters find that the difficulty of defending against attacks by the thoniks is increased by two steps (although a character who faints is automatically hit if targeted by a thonik).

The thonik presence suggests that the recursion has somehow been flayed open, allowing creatures of the Strange to enter it, perhaps at will. That's not a good thing.

THE CURIOUS CASE OF TOM MALLARD

You've already seen "The Curious Case of Tom Mallard" in *The Strange* corebook. If you haven't yet run it for your players, you could present it as one of the secondary missions of this adventure. Lead Operative Katherine Manners assigns two or more PCs to take a shift monitoring Tom Mallard, a recursion miner.

If you've already run "The Curious Case of Tom Mallard," no problem. That was the PCs' initial training mission. If they failed to capture Mallard (a.k.a. Tokmal the Master) at the adventure's end, it was probably because he escaped to Ruk, which means that when the PCs go to Ruk later in *The Dark Spiral* (see "Whole Body Grafts"), they might want to look for him there. That's fine, and a great way to provide continuity. On the other hand, if the PCs don't look for the Master, maybe he learns that the characters are in Ruk and shows up unexpectedly while they're investigating Semerimis Tower. How things fall out after that is up to you and your players.

Non-Estate PCs: The adventure in the corebook provides a couple of options for non-Estate PCs.

The Curious Case of Tom Mallard, page 386

Whole Body Grafts, page 65

Repercussions: If the PCs report what they've found (and especially if they fought thoniks), Hertzfeld makes a command decision to use his negation rifle on the gate to R639.

○●○● ▬▬▬▬▬
ARTIFACT: NEGATION RIFLE

Level: 1d6

Form: A broad-barreled rifle rich with embedded electronics

Effect: When the rifle is fired, a designated recursion gate (translation or inapposite) within short range collapses if it leads to a recursion whose level is equal to or less than the artifact's level. The recursion beyond the gate isn't otherwise affected.

Depletion: 1–2 in 1d10

●○○

○●○

MODIFYING A CREATURE'S LEVEL

When modifying a creature's level upward or downward to make it more suitable for characters of a particular tier, remember that several other statistics also vary with the level. Certainly a creature's level is a measure of its power, defense, intelligence, speed, and ability to interact with the world, but you also need to modify its health, damage, and Armor. One rule of thumb is as follows: for every level you add to (or subtract from) a creature, modify its health by 3 to 6 points, its damage by 1 or 2 points, and its Armor by 1 point. For every three levels you add to (or subtract from) a creature, add (or take away) one iteration of its standard attack that it can make during a single action.

●○○

MAIN ARC STARTING MISSION

What might seem to the PCs at first as just another mission for the Estate is actually one that connects directly to the main arc of *The Dark Spiral*: stop a drug dealer who sells spiral dust. The Estate rewards initial success by asking the PCs to roll up the entire spiral dust operation, which requires far more investment by the characters.

SPIRAL DUST DRUG BUST

Designer drugs are on the uptick, appearing on the street too quickly to be assessed and regulated by any official body. One of those is a drug called spiral dust. Though the drug bust mission begins like any other Estate-assigned mission, it could lead characters down an ever-more-dangerous path of investigation.

DRUG BUST MISSION BRIEFING

Investigations Chief Lawrence Keaton calls the PCs into a briefing room on the Estate campus for a new mission.

Keaton: The chief is looking bleary-eyed and ruffled, and even though Estate policy restricts alcohol on campus outside designated areas and lodging condos, he has a tumbler of scotch at his elbow. Though appearances might argue otherwise, Keaton remains on his game—for today, anyhow.

Mission Background: Keaton asks the PCs if they've heard of the street drug "spiral dust." Whether or not they have, he gets them up to speed by providing the following information through documents, photographs, and verbal explanation:

• The Estate believes that spiral dust is made from components gathered in another recursion or in the Strange itself—possibly from cyphers, though that hypothesis hasn't been confirmed.

• People who become addicted to spiral dust are called spiralers. Addicts are easy to spot: their hands tremble with excitement, their speech is exuberant, and, most telling of all, their irises change color, as if stained bluish-purple, and deform slightly as if taking on the shape of a fractal spiral. As a result, addicts usually wear sunglasses.

• Spiralers have incredibly vivid hallucinations while on the drug, and many of them believe that each drug trip is a continuing leg of their spiritual journey.

• Particularly heavy users of spiral dust sometimes disappear. It's hypothesized that such disappearances are either because an addict leaves behind her regular life to join a spiritual messiah in a distant compound, or because she dies of an overdose in an illicit drug den.

Mission Assignment: Keaton tells the PCs that they have solid intelligence about a local dealer, one LeRoy R. Cain. The PCs are to find Cain, shut him down, and discover whether he has a supplier or is "cooking" his own inventory. Keaton provides the following assets to help the PCs get started tracking Cain:

• A few pictures of Cain, revealing a tall man in a leather trench coat and a Stetson who is bearded, black haired, and blue eyed.

• A series of addresses that stretch from north of Seattle to far south, each a location where Cain has been seen dealing. Unfortunately, no one knows where he currently lives.

• A list of three suspected clients who buy from Cain, including their phone numbers and addresses: Melissa Romano, Sharon Coopersmith, and Eldridge Chopra.

• A document that assesses Cain's likelihood of being quickened: 90% likely.

• The contact number for the current Estate Fixer who will get the PCs out of any local

Spiral Dust Effects, page 36

The "Spiral Dust Drug Bust" mission is designed to serve as the lead-in to the larger adventure arc of The Dark Spiral.

The Fixer, page 149

legal entanglements if they run afoul of normal police during their mission.

The PCs are directed to warn Cain off. If he gives up his supplier or relinquishes the equipment and the method by which he procures spiral dust, the PCs can leave it at that, assuming they believe him. However, as quickened Estate operatives dealing with a presumably quickened enemy of Earth's interests, the PCs have wide latitude to deal with the situation as they believe best serves the organization's charter.

Before the PCs leave, Keaton gives each character a randomly determined cypher (if they need one to reach their cypher limit).

Non-Estate PCs: PCs hunting for cyphers find a small recursion that seems particularly rich with them. The recursion is one of the many created by fictional leakage and takes the form of a long beach facing a wide sea hidden by autumn mist. The surf always throws up a cypher or two during any given visit. During their visit to this recursion, the PCs run across another recursor, LeRoy R. Cain, who is beachcombing for cyphers, too. He reacts by attempting to lure the PCs into a confrontation with the dragon in the cave and then tries to use his cyphers to escape to Earth.

That's when the characters run into NPC operatives on LeRoy's trail. The operatives are either from the Estate, the Office of Strategic Recursion (OSR), or the Quiet Cabal. They explain their interest in rolling up the spiral dust trade and offer the PCs a limited contract to help them do so. Obviously, it'll be less work on the GM's part if the Estate is chosen as the contracting agency.

CAIN'S SPIRAL DUST CLIENTS

The PCs can follow up on one or more of the people who have been identified as clients of LeRoy Cain's drug trade.

Melissa Romano: Melissa works as a hair stylist in a swank Seattle salon. Or rather, she used to work there; she hasn't been to the salon for a week, and her peers assume she finally moved to Portland, Oregon, as she'd long threatened to do. If PCs call her apartment in Seattle, she doesn't answer, and if they go there, no one has been home for several days. Melissa is officially missing, and the trail is cold.

Sharon Coopersmith: Sharon is a freelance writer who has credits in online magazines and in newsprint, especially in the Northwest.

Show 'Em: *Effects of Spiral Dust, Image C, page 92*

Office of Strategic Recursion, page 157

Quiet Cabal, page 153

PCs can find her by calling the number provided by the Estate or by visiting her home, a rental house in the Queen Anne neighborhood of Seattle.

Sharon comes across as a bit scattered but essentially competent. If the PCs visit her in person, she wears shades even inside her apartment. If questioned about spiral dust, Sharon smiles and relates how it's the most wonderful thing. She says she "sees things differently now," and that "the world is a stranger place than you'd believe." (She wears shades because her irises have taken on a blue fractal swirl appearance; see "Spiral Dust Effects.")

Spiral Dust Effects, page 36

Sharon provides the PCs with the following information:

• She has a small stash of spiral dust, enough to last her for several months. She offers the PCs a single hit, if they'd like.

• She tells the PCs the cross-street address where she met a man in a leather trench coat (she never got a name) who sold her the dust. It's outside a warehouse where raves are sometimes held near the port. The address is *not* one the PCs already have for LeRoy Cain.

• Sharon knows three other people who take spiral dust, but she doesn't volunteer that information or tell the PCs their names without very strong reason. These acquaintances have stories similar to Sharon's.

Eldridge Chopra: Eldridge, or "Ridge" as his friends call him, works for one of the computer companies in Seattle that provide online auction services for whoever has something to sell. Eldridge got the idea to resell the spiral dust he bought from Cain under the name "Blue Rain" on an Internet auction site of the same name. However, Cain found out and had him killed. If the PCs track Eldridge down, it looks like he was the victim of a homicide on a street corner. The local police have no leads and have ascribed the murder to random gang violence.

Modifying a Creature's Level, page 16

FINDING LEROY CAIN

If the PCs stick with the addresses provided by their Estate briefing, they catch sight of LeRoy Cain after a few weeks of stakeouts. If the player characters are more proactive, either by trying to shake down the local drug dealers or by following up with Sharon Coopersmith, they learn of a location that Cain visits every few days: outside the rave warehouse that Sharon mentioned.

Of course, if the PCs shake up the local drug scene too much, LeRoy Cain becomes aware of them first. In that case (or if the PCs put out word that they're looking to buy spiral dust), LeRoy comes looking for them at a time and place of his choosing; see "LeRoy Sets a Trap," page 19.

CONFRONTING LEROY CAIN

If LeRoy is unaware of the PCs, they can confront him at one of his "places of sale." Regardless of the general area where they find him, when dealing, LeRoy prefers to loiter near a parking lot where his GMC Sierra pickup truck is parked. (It's not immediately obvious that the truck is his.)

Drug Deal: LeRoy is suspicious of any new customers who show up to buy spiral dust from him, but he still wants to make a sale. Unless the PCs actively blow their role as potential clients, he completes the sale of one or two doses ($50 per hit, but he can be wrangled down to $20). If the PCs place a larger order, LeRoy claims he'll have to make special arrangements first, which is true, but he is no fool—a big order from someone he doesn't know puts him on alert. Unless the PCs come up with a convincing reason for such an order, he either attacks them or sets a trap for them.

Modifying for Higher Tiers: If the characters' average tier is 3 or higher, increase LeRoy's level by 3. Regardless, PCs of tier 5 or higher probably won't have too much trouble dealing with LeRoy. See Modifying a Creature's Level for additional guidance.

LEROY CAIN	4 (12)

LeRoy is a tall man who is rarely without his signature black leather trench coat and Stetson. Bearded, black-haired, and with blue eyes like chips of ice, he cuts an imposing figure. LeRoy is a recursion miner and a dealer in spiral dust. Despite dealing, he isn't a user, which means his irises aren't fractally touched and his hands do not shake.

Motive: Acquire cash and cyphers

Health: 20

Damage Inflicted: 4 points

Armor: 1

Movement: Short

Modifications: Perception as level 6.

Combat: LeRoy is trained in unarmed combat but prefers to use the sawed-off shotgun concealed under his coat, which deals 6 points of damage to two targets next to each other in immediate range. LeRoy can fire his shotgun twice before he has to reload. On the other hand, he fights only if no other option presents itself. He first attempts to lie or flee, using some combination of his abilities and cyphers.

Fleet: LeRoy can move a short distance and take an action in the same round.

Lying: LeRoy can convince a PC who fails an Intellect defense roll of something wildly and obviously untrue for one round.

Translation: When LeRoy translates, he can choose to appear in a recursion as if he went through an inapposite gate.

Cyphers: LeRoy has a level 5 vanisher (which turns a user invisible for ten minutes), a level 5 curative (which restores 5 points of damage), and a level 3 temporary shield (which provides the user an asset to Speed defense rolls for one hour).

Interaction: LeRoy maintains a friendly facade. When challenged, he first tries to bully with a show of force (even deadly force), though if it becomes obvious that he is outmatched, he tries to get away from the conflict.

Loot: Cyphers listed under Combat, twelve shotgun shells, $340 in cash, five doses of spiral dust, the key fob for his GMC Sierra pickup truck, and a business card. The card is for an apartment building in Seattle's Pioneer Square neighborhood, and it has the words "apartment #27b" written on it.

Fighting LeRoy: LeRoy isn't too concerned about blazing away at people in the parking lot with his sawed-off shotgun, but if he faces more than two opponents, he knows the odds are not in his favor. He tries to get away after taking his first couple of shots, using his cypher that confers invisibility to good effect. If he manages to escape (and once he activates his cypher, he has a pretty good chance), all is not lost. He sets a trap for the PCs

in order to deal with the potential problem. If they somehow catch LeRoy before he can set a trap, see "What LeRoy Knows."

Trailing LeRoy: If the PCs find LeRoy and decide to trail him covertly instead of confront him, they have to succeed on a difficulty 6 stealth task every few hours so they don't tip him off (his high perception comes from years of working the streets with his eyes peeled for DEA or rival dealers). If LeRoy realizes that he is being trailed, he plays it cool until he can use his vanisher cypher to lose the PCs completely, then sets the trap as described below.

If LeRoy fails to notice the tail, the PCs eventually discover that he lives in the Crestview apartment complex in a Seattle neighborhood called Pioneer Square. If they catch him asleep in his room without his cyphers at hand, the characters might be able to bypass the trap, the trip to Oceanmist, and everything else, and learn the information in "What LeRoy Knows."

LEROY SETS A TRAP

If LeRoy learns about the PCs before they find him (or if they find him but he gets away), he goes into hiding and then sets a trap.

To bait the trap, LeRoy sends the PCs a postcard with his address, which is in a neighborhood called Pioneer Square. The address is in an apartment complex called Crestview. Crestview is ratty and not well maintained, and the PCs are able to walk right into the place without a key.

Apartment 27b: 27b is the apartment number scrawled on the postcard received from LeRoy. It's unlocked, and PCs who enter find a one-room suite that looks like it has been used for several months as a place for homeless people to sleep (and relieve themselves in corners). However, the place is empty of anyone at

What LeRoy Knows, page 22

Vanisher, page 331

Curative, page 315

Temporary shield, page 329

Pioneer Square: PC locals know that the area can be a bit rough, especially at night, because of the many bars and the active drug scene. Lone travelers might be accosted for their wallet, purse, or shoes.

C. Wilkins

the moment. If the PCs interview adjoining apartment tenants, the neighbors claim that apartment 27b is "haunted" and no one goes in there anymore. (The adjoining tenants include a family with several children, and a couple of college-age guys engrossed in a console video game.)

The PCs find two things of particular interest in 27b: a painting on the wall opposite the door, and a cypher duct-taped to the wall next to the painting.

LeRoy's Painting: The painting, displayed in a gold frame, is a well-rendered reproduction of a recursion LeRoy calls Oceanmist, where he often travels to collect cyphers.

Laws, page 136

read aloud

A beach stretches for miles down the coast, lit by a fractal-studded nightscape where massive spirals take the place of stars. Under this alien light, the surf sparkles with strange glints and glows. Not far back from the beach, a cave opening is visible. Mist seeps from the dark cavity.

The painting is so well rendered, in fact, that a quickened PC could use it to initiate a translation to the location shown (Oceanmist is level 3 for the purposes of translation).

Duct-Taped Cypher: LeRoy suspects that quickened agents of OSR or some other organization are after him, but he can't be sure that his pursuers have the ability to translate. So his trap has a backup designed to catch run-of-the-mill DEA agents. The cypher duct-taped to the wall has been partly activated (though that's not immediately clear through casual observation). The cypher is a recursion grenade (level 6) that explodes when removed from the wall, creating a momentary inapposite gate. Creatures within immediate range are sucked into Oceanmist.

When PCs travel through an inapposite gate, they don't translate, which means they don't gain new foci or equipment. Also, extreme laws like Magic and Mad Science also support the underlying baseline law of Standard Physics. Thus, equipment (and foci) brought through an inapposite gate from Earth doesn't degrade in those recursions unless specifically noted otherwise.

OCEANMIST

If the PCs follow the breadcrumbs into this recursion either by translating to it or by falling victim to the duct-taped grenade, they end up on the beach shown on the painting. The reality of the new recursion is similar to the painting in most ways, though the

Oceanmist
NOT TO SCALE

Ocean

Beach

Dragon's Lair

Tunnel

Footprints

Cave

LeRoy's Secret Camp

OCEANMIST ATTRIBUTES

Level: 3

Laws: Magic

Playable Races: Human

Foci: Entertains, Leads, Lives in the Wilderness, Slays Dragons, Wields Two Weapons at Once, Works Miracles

Skills: None

Connection to Strange: If one travels far enough into the ocean, the edge of the recursion is reached in a massive waterfall that empties into the Strange

Connection to Earth: A few gates

Size: A few miles (5 km) across

Spark: 0%

Trait: None

---

starscape is sometimes occluded by a massive moon. More immediately important, a set of footprints leads up to the cave mouth from which the mist pours.

Cave: Dropping quickened PCs into a recursion isn't enough to stop them, so LeRoy left footprints going into the cave entrance as an extension of his trap. Inside the entrance tunnel, the sand gives way to bare rock and floor-covering mist, making it impossible to see how much farther the tracks go. Presumably, they continue. In fact, LeRoy backtracked, left the cave, and retreated to his secret camp.

PCs who examine the area outside the cave for less obvious tracks are hampered by the seeping mist. Finding evidence of LeRoy's retreat requires a difficulty 5 Intellect-based roll. If found, the covert tracks lead to his secret camp.

Lair of the Hibernating Dragon: It's dark in the cave and a light source is required, though as soon as anyone enters, the sound of something snoring becomes audible over the crashing surf. The mist is thicker than ever in the cave, but PCs who travel all the way to the end of the winding tunnel (about 100 feet, or 30 m) can see the source of the snores: a 30-foot (9 m) long green-scaled dragon sleeps within a 50-foot (15 m) diameter cave.

The dragon sleeps on a bed of coins and cyphers, like any good dragon, but it doesn't rouse unless someone wakes it or filches from its hoard. If the PCs get on the good side of the dragon, it might offer them each one randomly determined cypher as a gift. If they

Dragon, page 267

The Oceanmist dragon has green scales, not feathers.

LeRoy is careful to shed any cyphers he carries before sifting for new ones along the beach. Even so, he loses a few on every haul. Laying claim to more than a small handful of cyphers at any one time, even if the cyphers are stored separately, is difficult if not impossible. Once more than a few cyphers are accumulated, extra cyphers have a tendency to dissipate spontaneously or slip away into another recursion. That doesn't keep LeRoy or other recursion miners from trying.

get on its bad side, it might hunt them down across the surface of Oceanmist, one by one.

Dragon Interaction: The dragon is more melancholy than mean unless physically attacked, whereupon it defends itself as only a dragon can. But otherwise it is detached and depressed, mainly from the lack of a playmate. Getting it to talk or answer questions (instead of just sigh sadly, shrug disinterestedly, or mumble something like "What does it matter, anyway?") is something of an effort.

One sure way the PCs can engage the dragon is by suggesting that they play a game. Dragons love games, and this one is no different. It perks right up for riddle games, Tic-Tac-Toe, jacks, cards, or any sort of game, and while playing, it relates the following to the PCs if they specifically ask:

• "I don't recall my name. It's been too long since anyone played with me. Call me what you like."

• "A man tried to steal from my hoard. I burned him a little, but I let him get away when he dropped what he'd stolen. He didn't want to play."

• "The thief has a camp nearby. Sometimes I can smell him cooking fish from the sea, even when I'm asleep."

• "I've thought about going out there and making the man play a game with me. But then I think, why bother? He'll just leave. Just like you'll leave, like everyone who's ever played with me has left, never to return."

Clever PCs might be able to convince the dragon to help them find or cow LeRoy if they make it part of a game or make promises of future visits, though the dragon won't actually attack LeRoy (unless attacked first) or leave the recursion of Oceanmist.

Leroy's Secret Camp: After LeRoy Cain laid down the false trail to the lair entrance, he carefully retreated to his camp, hidden by a press of palms about 100 feet (30 m) from the cave entrance. To find it, the PCs must blanket the area behind the palms or intentionally look for, find, and track LeRoy's real trail from the cave mouth.

The camp is filled with Earth gear because LeRoy set it up using his Translation ability. If the PCs have been tracking him, he is present at the camp, tending his fire (which is hidden by the press of trees), sleeping in his tent, or walking farther down the beach, depending on the time of day.

When the PCs confront LeRoy, refer to "What LeRoy Knows," below. If the PCs come to the camp and LeRoy isn't there (and won't be returning), they can search the camp and learn the same information to move the adventure forward.

The camp includes a tent filled with basic camping gear, a fire pit, a lawn chair, and a cooler with the latest cyphers that LeRoy gathered on the beach. In addition to a good amount of sand, the cooler contains three cyphers, all level 3. These fractal-shaped seashells convey the following effects:

• Restores 1d6 + 3 points to the user's Might Pool.

• Increases the user's Speed Edge by 1.

• Allows the user to breathe water for 24 hours after activation.

The Beach: Each hour the PCs spend combing the beach for cyphers gives one of them the opportunity to make a difficulty 6 Intellect-based roll to perceive a random cypher tossed up by the surf. No matter how long the PCs search or how well they roll, the beach throws up a maximum of seven cyphers each week.

WHAT LEROY KNOWS

LeRoy puts up a show fight if the PCs confront him in his secret camp, but in the end, he would much rather surrender than die. As a show of good faith, he provides the PCs with the following information, plus all the hits of spiral dust he still has with him.

• "Hey, I'm just making a living here!"

• "The dust is made in Colorado. That's where my supplier lives, anyhow. I never met her, only talked to her on the phone. Goes by the name of Lydia. Lydia Nance."

• "Lydia sends me a 'care package' of spiral dust every month or so through USPS. Usually not enough for the demand, but apparently, she only has so much."

• "I don't know if she's the ultimate source or not. She's *my* ultimate source, and I don't know anyone else who deals.

• "Lydia works at a gem shop in Nederland, Colorado. I got her card right here—you can have it." (If the PCs incapacitate LeRoy so that he is unable to answer their questions, he leaves behind a business card for the Dreaming Crystal rock and gem shop in Nederland, Colorado. Scrawled on the back is the name "Lydia Nance.")

• "Actually, some other woman gave me my first hit of spiral dust to sell. It was night, raining hard, and I didn't really get a good look at her. I never found out her name. I assume she worked for Nance." (In fact, that first contact was Uentaru in translated human form, scouting for quickened recursors who could push her product without worry of entanglements from regular Earth authorities.)

INTERMISSIONS

As the characters carry out their investigations that are part of the main arc, they'll likely return to the Estate campus to conduct research, rest, and request additional resources. During these periods, intermissions can occur, according to the variable timing described for each.

INTERMISSION 1: ZOMBIES!

As the PCs begin to roll up the spiral dust trade on Earth, reports of their progress by various observers reach Uentaru. Concerned that the characters might eventually figure out what she's up to, she asks the Dustman to eliminate them. However, that turns out to be something of a mistake because the Dustman isn't a servitor of Uentaru, only an ally of convenience. Rather than quietly eliminate the PCs, the Dustman "activates" the minds of spiral dust addicts and sends them, zombielike, to attack the Estate headquarters when the PCs are present.

Non-Estate PCs: The zombie incursion described in this section could be adapted to occur in nearly any location.

Modifying for Higher Tiers: For each tier the characters' average tier is above 2, add one zombie to each group of zombies that targets them. If the PCs are tier 5 or higher, add two zombies to each group. If the PCs' average tier is 3 or higher, increase the level of all the zombies by 2.

TIMING FOR INTERMISSION 1

Intermission 1 could occur in a few places during the timeline of the larger adventure.

After Nederland: Once the PCs take care of Lydia Nance and her Dreaming Crystal rock shop in "Never, Nederland," they could return to the Estate campus to research Donna Ilsa or request aid for translating to Crow Hollow. Intermission 1 could occur just before they translate to that recursion (possibly even interrupting the translation trance).

Before or During "Mouth of Swords": If the PCs return to the Estate after accepting Donna Ilsa's proposal or at any point while

---

● ○ ● ▬▬▬▬▬▬▬

WHAT TO DO WITH LEROY?

The PCs are not law enforcement and are not responsible for taking LeRoy off the street for his crimes. First and foremost, the Estate wants them to find the source of the spiral dust, so LeRoy's primary importance is as someone who can finger his supplier. On the other hand, the PCs are Estate operatives tasked with opposing threats to Earth that stem from the Strange. LeRoy Cain certainly qualifies, which gives the characters justification for nearly any solution they devise, up to and including eliminating LeRoy. Less bloodthirsty PCs can have the Estate put him in Holding for up to a month while they pursue the leads he provided. But warning him off and stopping the drug supply upstream could also be considered enough.

▬▬▬▬▬▬▬ **● ○ ○**

---

attempting to retrieve the eggs from the Mouth of Swords, Intermission 1 could occur.

After Intermission 2: It's possible that the PCs meet Uentaru (in Intermission 2) before Intermission 1 happens. Despite coming across as an ally, she could still instruct the Dustman to take the PCs out—probably in an attempt to stop them from journeying to the center of the Earth.

1. ADDICTS GATHER

In addition to the other consequences of addiction to spiral dust, an addict also leaves herself open to "activation" by the Dustman, a mysterious figure intimately associated with the production of the material.

A spiral dust addict who has been partially activated by the Dustman becomes open to suggestion for several hours or days, but can revert to normal afterward with no memory of what she did during the period of activation. Partially activated addicts "present" (to use the clinical term) like someone strung out on hallucinogens (or spiral dust) and thus are not particularly versatile in what they can accomplish. On the other hand, they can pass as regular, if slightly bewildered, people.

The Dustman launches a zombie attack on the Estate campus by partially activating the closest hundred spiral dust addicts (which means the net extends across several states) and gathering them in a location near the campus, such as a park or other public area. When he sees or gets confirmation that the

Uentaru, page 81

Dustman, page 82

Mouth of Swords, page 47

Never, Nederland, page 30

PCs are on the campus, he sends a busload of addicts posing as lost, befuddled tourists onto the grounds.

read aloud

A surprising number of people are out and about on campus. Most of them lack the purposeful gait that marks an operative. In fact, these people almost look like tourists who are lost, if their confused expressions and bewildered body language is anything to go by.

2. ZOMBIES ATTACK

PCs on campus can learn about the zombie attack in a couple of different ways. The most visceral way is for the characters to serve as the catalyst for the attack as they move between buildings (perhaps on the way to or from Lodging). They also might witness the first attack through a surveillance camera.

read aloud

A change sweeps across all the visitors, including several dozen bystanders just visible beyond the edges of the campus. They kick and shudder, and a few fall down as if in the grip of a seizure. When they stop shaking, they're different. Instead of confusion, hunger and rage are scrawled across their snarling faces. As if of one mind, they shamble forward.

The zombies attacking the Estate are quickened, which means that their eyes glow with blue-purple light and they are resistant to the special abilities of other quickened creatures. Once completely activated, there's no going back from being a zombie. Luckily, quickened zombies are not infectious, though the PCs might not know this (and might assume the opposite).

3. SURVIVING A ZOMBIE HORDE

The characters can't fight off a hundred or more zombies by themselves. But they don't have to; they're at the Estate, which employs armed security and has other quickened operatives.

To make it possible for the PCs to survive, throw groups of no more than five to six zombies at them at any one time. All in all, they might fight a total of twenty or so zombies during the horde attack; these battles can be part of a series of skirmishes set to a backdrop of other Estate operatives and employees fighting for their lives all around

them.

Elements to incorporate in the conflict include the following options, some of which you could treat as GM intrusions.

Jenkins! At a location just beyond long range, one or more PCs see a horde of twenty or more zombies descend on valiant but doomed Jenkins, an Estate security guard. The creatures grab him and basically pull his head off, abruptly ending his screams.

Barricade Breaks: To escape a wave of thirty or more zombies, the PCs run into the nearest structure (perhaps the Lodging building's lobby) and barricade the door. However, after a few rounds, the barricade breaks and zombies pour through at an alarming rate. The characters must retreat further or stand their ground and fight.

Area Not Safe: While retreating, the PCs find an area they believe is safe. However, they learn the error of their ways when a previously hidden zombie sits up and bites a PC on the ankle.

Security Squad: A group of ten Kevlar-wearing, helmeted Estate guards emerges from the Security building and begins tasering zombies, which seems to short-circuit their brains, leaving them breathing but unmoving. (Tasered zombies rise again within 24 hours.) Unfortunately, one of the PCs is mistaken for a zombie and must succeed against a difficulty 5 Might-based attack or take 5 points of damage from electricity and be stunned and unable to act for one round.

Isn't That Sharon? One or more of the PCs encounter an NPC they've previously met in connection with the spiral dust mission: Sharon Coopersmith (or another NPC who they know to have taken spiral dust). For one PC who is especially surprised, the difficulty of a Speed defense roll against the NPC's attack is increased by one step.

Katherine Manners and Hertzfeld Kick Ass: Just when it seems that a flood of thirty or more zombies is about to wash over the PCs, Katherine Manners and Hertzfeld distract a large portion of the invaders with explosives, leading them off so the PCs have to deal with only four or five—at least for that moment.

The Dustman: A PC sees a dreamy image of the Dustman observing the fight—a shadowy, hooded figure. If they previously caught sight of the Dustman or heard a description of him, they might recognize him. Otherwise, the shadowed, humanoid shape is a new development. The observing PC must succeed

at a difficulty 4 Intellect defense roll or see the burning sapphire eyes (not unlike those of a zombie) within the shadow, which earns her a round of inactivity due to the dreamlike command those eyes elicit. A round later, the Dustman image is gone.

Wrapping up the Attack: As a suggestion, stop throwing new zombies at the PCs once at least one character is impaired. The PCs should feel truly threatened but not risk eradication. As the characters conclude their last zombie skirmish, they notice that other operatives and security squads are doing the same, leaving the campus quiet but littered with unmoving forms.

ZOMBIE   3 (9)

Humans transformed into aggressive, hard-to-kill serial killers with no memory of their former existence are called zombies. Depending on a zombie's recursion of origin, the reason for its transformation varies and might be an undead curse, a psychic possession, an AI meatware overwrite, a viral infection, a drug overdose, or something else. Regardless of how the transformation happened, the result is much the same on every world where zombies roam: a creature whose humanity has been burned out and replaced with unquenchable hunger.

Zombies aren't intelligent, but enough of them together sometimes exhibit emergent behavior, just as ants can coordinate activities across a colony. Thus, zombies alone or in small groups aren't an overwhelming threat for someone who has a baseball bat or can get away. But it's never wise to laugh off a zombie horde.

Motive: Hunger (for flesh, cerebrospinal fluid, certain human hormones, and so on)

Environment (Magic, Mad Science, Psionics, or Standard Physics): Almost anywhere, in groups of five or six, or in hordes of tens to hundreds

Health: 12

Damage Inflicted: 3 points

Movement: Immediate

Modifications: Speed defense as level 2.

Combat: Zombies never turn away from a conflict. They fight on, no matter the odds, usually attacking by biting, but sometimes by tearing with hands made into claws by the erosion of skin over their finger bones.

When zombies attack in groups of five to seven individuals, they can attack a single target as a group, making a single attack roll as one level 5 creature, inflicting 5 points of damage.

Zombies are hard to finish off. If an attack

Show 'Em: Dustman Observing, Image D, page 92

would reduce a zombie's health to 0, it does so only if the number rolled by the attack was an even number; otherwise, the zombie is reduced to 1 point of health instead. This might result in a dismembered, gruesomely damaged zombie that is still moving.

GM Intrusion: *Even after the PC kills the zombie, it doesn't die. In fact, treat the zombie as if it had 12 more points of health.*

Zombies can see in the dark at short range. "Fresh" zombies are vulnerable to electricity. The first time a zombie takes 5 or more points of damage from an electrical attack, it falls limp and unmoving. Assuming nothing interferes with the process, the zombie arises minutes or hours later without the vulnerability.

Some zombies have special additional qualities, including being quickened.

Quickened: A zombie that "rises" from a quickened human (or a zombie born of a normal person addicted to spiral dust) resists attacks gained from focus abilities, revisions, twists, and moves as a level 5 creature. A quickened zombie's eyes (or empty sockets) glow with purplish fire.

Interaction: Zombies groan when they see something that looks tasty. They do not reason, cannot speak, and never stop pursuing something they've identified as a potential meal, unless something else edible comes closer.

Use: The characters are asked to clear out the basement of a mad scientist, necromancer, or psychic surgeon, or possibly an old military depot on Earth. The appearance of zombies probably comes as an unpleasant surprise.

ZOMBIE AFTERMATH

The PCs survived. Now it's time to pick up the pieces and try to make sense of what happened.

Immediate Aftermath: PCs who want to help clean up are welcomed. Immediate needs include:

• Find wounded people and provide first aid.

• Eliminate lone zombie stragglers (a few managed to get stuck in closets, caught with their ankle in a gutter, or slammed in a door).

• Help identify and transfer electrically zapped but still breathing zombies to Holding.

• Help identify and transfer dead zombies to a special inapposite gate in the Gate House used for waste disposal (which opens into a recursion of burning fire).

• Help Hertzfeld transfer two or three specimens to his lab, located beneath the Recursion Lab building.

• Anything else the PCs decide is important.

Eight Hours Later: Katherine Manners calls the PCs into a briefing room along with several other staff and operatives who participated in the fight, including Hertzfeld and Lawrence Keaton. Manners calls the meeting to order and asks for a report. An NPC agent named Connolly reads from an after-zombie report. Depending on how things transpired, it's possible that PC activities led to one or more of the presented points. The PCs are also asked to give their own report.

After-Zombie Report

• Twelve dead staff, with twenty-four injured (three seriously).

• Hertzfeld's tests show that the zombies don't seem infectious "unlike on TV," which is lucky.

• Several operatives reported seeing a "shadowy figure in a hood" during the attack. The Estate records have no information on such a presence, so Manners sent out feelers to special individuals the Estate has used in the past as consultants on entities from the Strange. Results of this inquiry are pending. (Uentaru is one of the consultants.)

• Hertzfeld's preliminary tests indicate that the zombies were spiral dust-maddened people whose past consumption of the drug left them vulnerable to the transformation. Hertzfeld is happy to talk more about these results, but he doesn't know how much spiral dust one must have consumed to be vulnerable. PCs who have sampled the dust *might* have reason to worry, he cautions.

• Though the zombies were opportunistic when it came to targets, they seemed most drawn to the PCs.

• One last, troubling thing: Hertzfeld notes that the zombies—as well as regular people high on a hit of spiral dust—exhibit qualities of quickened creatures. It's as if while experiencing the effects of a dose, an addict gains abilities (and drawbacks) identical to those possessed by quickened creatures. Once the effect of a dose lapses, the user ceases to exhibit these characteristics. Hertzfeld wants to do more tests, but given the potential for zombification of addicts, it's probably best to suspend investigation on that front for the moment.

The Upshot: Whatever else comes of the after-zombie report, one thing is clear: putting an end to the spiral dust trade is far more important than first imagined. The PCs are enjoined to get cracking. At this point, the free handout of one cypher to each PC begins to dry up, but the characters are offered three anoetic cyphers to split among the group: a level 5 Strange ammunition clip (cold), a level 6 Strange ammunition clip (fire), and a level 7 Strange ammunition clip (poison).

INTERMISSION 2: MEET UENTARU

Uentaru eventually becomes aware of the PCs, and when her early attempt to stop the characters backfires (Intermission 1), she decides that the best way to end their meddling is by infiltrating the group. It's possible she's given that opportunity under the guise of a special consultant called in to advise the PCs regarding the Dustman and the quickened zombies that attacked during Intermission 1.

Non-Estate PCs: The characters can meet Uentaru as they prepare to storm Whole Body Grafts in Ruk, where she pretends to be a victim who needs to be rescued (possibly from a surgical theater or one of the areas inside Nakarand).

Modifying for Higher Tiers: Intermission 2 probably won't include combat. However, if the PCs somehow see through Uentaru's facade and they are fifth- or sixth-tier characters, increase her level by 3. See Modifying a Creature's Level (page 16) for additional guidance.

TIMING FOR INTERMISSION 2

Intermission 2 could occur in a few places during the course of the larger adventure.

Immediately After Intermission 1: During Intermission 1, at least one PC and several NPCs witnessed the Dustman. It's possible that the consultant called in to help (Uentaru) arrives so quickly that the PCs haven't moved on to another part of the adventure yet.

After the Mouth of Swords: Most likely, Intermission 2 occurs when (or if) the PCs head back to the Estate after returning Donna Ilsa's eggs (page 46) to prepare for translating to Ruk.

Summoned by Courier: A courier arrives with a message requesting that the PCs return to the Estate to talk to a new consultant who has important information. (A couple of NPC agents who act as couriers have a special ability to track down other Estate operatives. The fine print of the PCs' employment agreement opted them in to this service, but now that they know about it, they can opt out so they can't be tracked in the future.)

Never: Uentaru prefers to infiltrate the Estate's efforts to shut down the spiral dust trade, but she might fail to make the connection. In this case, she seeks to join the PCs at another location—possibly as they face the dangers of the Vengeance-class battle chrysalid in "Whole Body Grafts."

CONFERENCE

The PCs are called to a conference in one of the meeting rooms on the Estate campus. If any of them have a supervising officer other than Katherine Manners or Hertzfeld, that SO is also present in the room.

read aloud

Doughnuts, coffee, and a vegetable tray are laid out on the conference room table. Three people eating and engaged in quiet conversation are gathered around the table. Two you recognize: Lead Operative Katherine Manners and Research Chief Hertzfeld. The third is a tall woman with short-cropped blonde hair. Despite her black jeans, blouse, and stylish yellow jacket, her physique and posture betray a military background.

Strange ammunition, page 328

Uentaru, page 81

Whole Body Grafts, page 65

Uentaru's Real Plan, page 80

Uentaru (Earth context): level 6; health 18; Armor 1; all deception tasks as level 8; long-range, high-caliber pistol that inflicts 7 points of damage; cyphers: level 6 transvolution, level 5 vanisher; artifact: level 6 communicator

Transvolution, page 330

Vanisher, page 331

Earth's Connection to the Strange, page 148

Abeyance, page 129

UENTARU'S FACADE

Uentaru comes across as friendly, helpful, and concerned, but this is an act to hide her true plans. A masterful deceiver, she is able to fool others (and often herself) as if level 8. Much of what she reveals during Intermission 2 is true, but it isn't the whole picture. For her true goals and motivations, see Uentaru's Real Plan.

The tall woman with military bearing is introduced as Ambassador Uentaru (pronounced "oo-en-TAR-oo"), a consultant the Estate has used in the past when dealing with the Strange. After a few pleasantries, she gives a short presentation, and then the PCs and Uentaru can quiz each other before deciding on the next steps.

1. PLEASANTRIES

The PCs learn the following about Uentaru as they gather around the table to help themselves to snacks. The information is provided by the Estate staff present or by Uentaru in answer to questions they pose. The information is mostly true, up to a point.

• *Origin:* Ambassador Uentaru is a native of the universe of normal matter. She isn't from Earth but rather an alien civilization hundreds of thousands of light years from Earth.

• *Homeworld:* Uentaru's world, Mycaeum, was not as lucky as Earth. Like every other realm she's come across in her travels, it was destroyed about a thousand years ago by planetovores.

• *Fled her world's destruction:* Uentaru was a sort of military scientist among her own kind. She escaped into the Chaosphere thanks to advanced technology she commanded. Able to save herself, she could only watch in horror and shame as her civilization was consumed by a planetovore. Lest she become caught up in the end of her world, she had to turn away and flee across the dark energy network.

• *Does good works:* She'd like to redeem her destroyed homeworld. One way she does so is by helping other survivors. Now that she has discovered Earth and the Estate, she wants to help the organization learn more about the Chaosphere.

• *Lives in the Chaosphere:* Uentaru normally lives in the Strange at a location called the Embassy of Uentaru. With her are other alien survivors from across the universe who share her goals. The group's name translated to English is "Chaos Templars," and as the name suggests, individual templars adventure across the infinite expanse of the Strange, always looking for ways to stem the planetovore threat.

• *Fascinated by Earth's special connection to the Strange:* People on Earth, even those who are quickened, probably don't realize how special their planet is. Unlike any place Uentaru has ever visited before, Earth has a special relationship to the Chaosphere. One of her projects is to discover why. She throws out a wild supposition that sometime during the Earth's late heavy bombardment four billion years ago, perhaps a massive object hit the planet, forming the moon. Maybe that object is somehow resonating with the dark energy network.

(Truth is, Uentaru *knows* that such an object is embedded in the Earth—something she calls the Aleph component, a small piece of a defunct alien intergalactic transport system; for more details, see Earth's Connection to the Strange in the corebook. Uentaru doesn't reveal all she knows at this time. She wants to see what the Estate knows and how close they might be to understanding her real plan.)

2. UENTARU'S PRESENTATION

The ambassador has a few things to say regarding spiral dust and the Dustman.

• *Spiral dust origin:* Spiral dust isn't made of ground-up cyphers or processed violet spiral as the Estate has postulated, at least not in any way that Uentaru has been able to reverse-engineer.

• *Creating quickened creatures:* Spiral dust use can temporarily give a normal creature, even one without the spark, limited abilities as if the user were quickened. For the period of time the drug is in a creature's system, it actually *is* quickened. (Hertzfeld may have already discovered this.)

• *Dreams are partial translations:* The intense dreams of a heavy user represent the user's dream self appearing in a random recursion during the sleep period. The user's sleeping body does not go into abeyance.

• *Overdose results in one-way translation:* The user disappears because instead of his dream self appearing in a random recursion, he fully translates against his will and is deposited in a mysterious recursion. The nature of that recursion is something that Uentaru has spent much time investigating, with no success. (In fact, she knows that addicts are drawn to

Nakarand, page 73

● ○ ●

MYCAEUM

Not much is known about this long-vanished world, given that Uentaru is its only purported survivor. If asked, she describes it thusly: "Great cities of slender spires reached past Mycaeum's golden sky, all the way to orbit, glistening in the glory of three suns. A great people lived there and on nearby planets in our solar system before they were consumed."

● ○ ●

Nakarand, though she doesn't reveal that at this time.)

• *The Dustman and spiral dust are connected:* An entity she calls the Dustman is somehow connected to spiral dust and the drug's users. Sometimes users describe seeing the Dustman in their dreams: a shadowy figure in a hood, usually without features, though sometimes with points of sapphire fire for eyes.

• *The Dustman can control addicts:* Evidence suggests that the Dustman can control the minds of addicts through some kind of psychic connection. Those so controlled seem fully in the grip of a spiral dust trip, which means they aren't as dangerous as they could be. Once released, addicts can't remember anything that happened during the preceding period.

• *Zombification of addicts:* If the Dustman completely activates a spiral dust addict, the addict "dies" and a quickened zombie is born, intent on achieving the last command imparted by the Dustman. This last point angers Uentaru, but probably not for the reasons the characters believe. She is angered because the Dustman sent such zombies against the PCs, which endangered her plan, and because zombies are much less quickened than spiral dust addicts. They don't provide the same kind of density of quickened creatures she needs to achieve her real goal.

3. QUESTIONS

The PCs and other Estate operatives are encouraged to ask Uentaru questions, and Uentaru to do the same of them.

• *The Dustman must be stopped!* If it's not already clear, Uentaru attempts to set the Dustman up as the villain behind everything the PCs have been investigating. (She leaves out the fact that she has been working with the Dustman to spread spiral dust use on Earth.)

• *What have you been up to?* Uentaru doesn't want to come across as desperate to know what the PCs have learned, though she asks details about their adventures and proves a great listener.

4. NEXT STEPS

Once general questions are out of the way, it's time for Uentaru to leave and for the PCs to move on. But she has a parting gift for the characters: an artifact she calls a communicator. When the PCs need her, they shouldn't hesitate to call, and she'll answer any questions they have or, if the need is dire, translate to them as quickly as she can arrange.

If the PCs are ready to head to Ruk now, Uentaru offers herself as a consultant and companion. She says she wants to see what Donna Ilsa's "supplier" has to do with the Dustman. If the PCs have already linked the two, she says it's one of her best leads regarding the Dustman, and she'd likely go there on her own if the PCs don't want her in their group.

After the conference, Lawrence Keaton suggests dinner and drinks to celebrate the partnership, but unless Uentaru is convinced otherwise, she is unwilling to engage in such frivolous behavior when "the Dustman is out there, plotting."

Finally, the PCs are offered two anoetic cyphers that they can split among them: a level 5 stim and a level 7 curative.

Stim, page 328

Curative, page 315

● ○ ●

ARTIFACT: COMMUNICATOR

Level: 1d6 + 2

Form: Two matched fossil-like spirals

Effect: A communicator is a special artifact of the Strange that travels between recursions when its user translates without losing its abilities.

The artifact comes in two pieces. Whoever holds one piece can activate it and verbally communicate with the owner of the matched piece for up to one minute per use. The communication is instantaneous and works at any range, even across recursions.

Special Effect: Each piece also serves as a recursion key, allowing a quickened creature to translate to the location of the other piece (but otherwise following the normal rules of translation). This special effect isn't obvious even to those who know the artifact's main effect.

Depletion: 1 in 1d100

● ○ ●

Recursion key, page 130

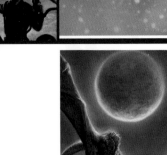

NEVER, NEDERLAND

This adventure is part of the main arc of The Dark Spiral *and is appropriate for PCs who learned about the Nederland rock shop during the drug bust mission in the last chapter. As a stand-alone scenario, "Never, Nederland" offers the characters a chance to temporarily disrupt the worldwide trade of spiral dust, put a stop to disappearing homeless people, and travel to the recursion of Crow Hollow, potentially the most diverse market in the Shoals of Earth.*

BACKGROUND

A drug called spiral dust is being used and abused in a few relatively small and scattered locations across the globe. The entire supply of drug flows from one place: Nederland, Colorado, USA. In particular, the drug issues from a tiny Nederland gift shop called the Dreaming Crystal. The operation is secret and relies on shop owner Lydia Nance, who acts as an intermediary for the drug flow because she fears for her own life if she doesn't cooperate.

Lydia Nance is a front for Donna Ilsa, the head of a mafia family in Crow Hollow. But like Lydia, Donna Ilsa also has a supplier of spiral dust, a mysterious figure she knows as the Dustman. The Dustman, though, doesn't play favorites, and also supplies Ilsa's main adversary, Don Wyclef, thus plunging the streets of Crow Hollow into a mafia family gang war.

Lydia Nance: level 4; 9mm pistol inflicts 4 points of damage at long range; key ring has a key to the shop and another to the basement

SYNOPSIS

The PCs follow clues that lead them to a rock shop in Colorado. Investigating the shop reveals that monstrous spiders nest in the basement and that the owner, Lydia Nance, occasionally feeds them homeless people she has lured from the streets of Boulder. If the PCs defeat her, they can discover that her spiral dust supplier is someone called Donna Ilsa.

With research, the PCs learn that Donna Ilsa is a native of Crow Hollow. After translating there, the PCs have a chance to shop at a recursion-spanning market and pursue Ilsa. While dodging drug violence, the characters might learn that both Don Wyclef and Donna Ilsa are making bank selling spiral dust in the Glittering Market (but only Ilsa is selling on Earth). Both do so to fund their efforts against the other.

Don Wyclef isn't interested in any sort of compromise that involves giving up his supply of spiral dust. Gang war or no, it's too valuable.

On the other hand, for all her bloodthirstiness, Donna Ilsa offers the PCs a deal. If they sneak into an Ardeyn location called the Mouth of Swords and safely retrieve her eggs (which were kidnapped a year ago), she will not only give up the trade but also tell them the location of the facility that processes spiral dust.

GETTING THE PCs INVOLVED

The most straightforward way to bring the PCs into this adventure is by having the Estate assign it to them as operatives, especially if they brought in LeRoy Cain. If that doesn't work out, try the following option.

Non-Estate PCs: No one keeps very good track of homeless people, but Boulder, Colorado, has more than its share of them thanks to progressive programs and services the city provides. Several homeless people have disappeared lately. Local law doesn't seem particularly concerned, but aid worker Marcus Winfrey *is* concerned. Though not a particularly brave man, he kept a close eye on people who used the services of his shelter. His scrutiny paid off: he saw a woman in a green Bronco drive up, offer a ride to Rosa Wilkins (who accepted), and drive off. That was the last Marcus ever saw of Rosa. The police remain uninterested, so Marcus advertises more widely and manages to contact the PCs. He shows them a picture he snapped of the car. The plates are too blurred to make out, but one sticker on the back says, "Nedhead and proud," and another proclaims, "Geodes and more: Dreaming Crystal rock shop has it all!"

MODIFYING FOR DIFFERENT TIERS

It's likely that the PCs have only one encounter of note while on Earth during "Never, Nederland," and that's with the night spiders nesting in the basement of the rock shop. For every tier the characters' average tier is above 2, add one more night spider to the mix. If the PCs are fifth- or sixth-tier characters, increase the level of the night spiders by 2.

If the PCs travel to Crow Hollow and are fourth tier, increase the level of all the kro goons, elite kro goons, and kro coursers by 2. If the PCs are fifth- or sixth-tier characters, increase the level of all the kro goons, elite kro goons, and kro coursers by 4.

NEDERLAND, COLORADO

Just west of Boulder, Colorado, up a winding, canyon-walled road lies Nederland. It's not the average small town, beginning with the fact that it's perched reasonably high in the Rocky Mountains (elevation: 8,230 feet [2.5 km]). Filled with small shops, sightseeing opportunities, and a vibrant music scene, the town sees far more traffic than might be expected considering that it has a population just shy of 2,000.

People in Nederland call themselves "Nedheads" because visitors are less likely to impress them with a Lexus and more likely to impress them with knowledge of foraging for certain kinds of mushrooms or the best telemark ski routes on the nearby peaks visible from most anywhere in town.

Traveling to Nederland: The PCs can request travel arrangements through their supervising officer and, with hardly any red tape, find themselves bound for Denver International Airport, with a rental car or two waiting at the terminal and reservations at the Residence Suites in Boulder (a college town that lies in the foothills west of Nederland) or in Nederland itself at the Best Western Lodge.

RESEARCHING THE ROCK SHOP

Nederland's Dreaming Crystal rock and gem shop is easily found with a web search. The shop has a website, though it was apparently created in the late 1990s and never updated, as it provides only minimal information, which includes a physical address in Nederland, a phone number, and a few pictures of semiprecious gemstones. Each photo is captioned with a New Age sentiment about how this or that jewel will revitalize health, restore vitality, or supercharge libido. Anyone wishing to purchase any of these alluring offerings is invited to stop in or call. The site has no ecommerce option, and hacking it leads to no further information.

Calling ahead (whether using the number on LeRoy's card or finding it in a web search) always triggers an answering service in a woman's voice that gives the hours of operation (9 to 6 Monday to Saturday, closed Sundays) and asks the caller to leave a message, which will be returned. A week after getting the PCs' message, shop employee Everett Rand finally calls them back (unless they visit the shop in the meantime) and is happy to arrange a sale. Rand knows nothing about spiral dust but everything about geodes.

DREAMING CRYSTAL SHOP

The shop is a single-story structure on one of the few main streets in Nederland.

read aloud

A large sign decked out in flecks of glittering mica overhangs the storefront and reads "Dreaming Crystal Rock and Gem Shop: Find Your Dream Here!" The front of the shop features a large plate glass window, behind which you see all manner of geodes, crystals, polished minerals, and both rough and polished fossils.

Surveilling the Shop: Visual surveillance of the Dreaming Crystal reveals that customers come and go during normal business hours, mostly coming from Boulder to visit the quaint mountain shop in the quaint mountain town (though some travel from much farther away). When customers purchase items, it's never spiral dust.

Delsey Robinson: level 2, level 4 for all tasks involving skiing, rock climbing, and related mountain activities

Everett Rand: level 2, level 4 for all tasks involving identifying and explaining geological features

The Fixer, page 149

Cleaning service professional: level 2, level 4 for all tasks related to cleaning

Nederland police officer: level 3; health 9; Armor 2; pistol deals 4 points of damage at long range

The staff consists of two people, Delsey Robinson and Everett Rand. Delsey Robinson is a woman in her twenties with many superlative tattoos who takes frequent clove cigarette breaks along the side street. Everett Rand is a thin, white-bearded man who is never without his battered Fedora hat. He is an expert self-taught geologist and waxes geologic with the least excuse.

The owner, Lydia Nance, is a woman always dressed in a fashionable business suit, but she rarely shows up in the front of the shop except as necessary to move from the entrance to the back hallway. She spends most of her time in back, presumably in the office.

Every day, a shipping service drops off several packages of new stock and picks up about as many (fulfillment of merchandise sold over the phone).

Two cleaning service professionals show up once a day and clean the main shop, the hallway, and the bathroom. They don't have keys for anything else.

Investigating the Staff: The staff and owner go home each night to separate homes. Delsey rooms with friends in a nearby Nederland house, Everett has a home in a nearby mountain town called Gold Hill, and Lydia lives down in Boulder in a moderately sized house in an old neighborhood.

Delsey and Everett are the innocents they seem to be and know nothing about spiral dust. They have only positive things to say about Lydia. The only thing out of the ordinary that either can come up with, and only if pressed, is that Lydia keeps the stairs to the basement locked and has said that going down there would probably get them killed. Both assumed she was joking.

During regular interaction, Lydia seems like a cordial professional, happy to talk shop on almost any topic but one. If questioned about spiral dust, her manner changes; see "Lydia Talks About Spiral Dust."

Shop Security: The locks on the front and side doors of the shop are level 5. Of course, a rock through the window would provide instant access. But entering without deactivating the security system (a difficulty 5 Intellect-based task) trips a screaming, flashing shop alarm.

The alarm summons two Nederland police officers, who pull up in a vehicle within five minutes. The police are trained professionals and arrest any thieves they find breaking into the shop. If they encounter resistance, they call in a dozen more officers on their radios, who arrive within a half hour. The best bet for PCs taken into custody is to use their one call to contact the Estate's Fixer.

What's Really Going On: About one in ten packages shipped out by the gem shop contains twenty doses of spiral dust. Lydia prepares all normal items sold through the shop in the privacy of her office, and it's easy to slip shipments of spiral dust into the regular flow of parcels without anyone being the wiser. The spiral dust packages go out to various dealers around the world. LeRoy Cain was just one recipient.

SHOP

read aloud

Shelves and displays overflow with lapidary equipment, mineral specimens, sea shells, finished jewelry, geodes, crystals of every mineral under the sun, and many "one-of-a-kind" gifts, including postcards of scenic Nederland. One wall holds a wide counter with a glass display front of especially interesting geologic specimens, mostly fossils.

During store hours, the shop has about six customers at any one time, as well as Delsey and Everett. The shop normally carries several thousand dollars' worth of stock and has a few hundred dollars in the cash register. The displays are locked, but Delsey and Everett have keys (to the displays and to the shop itself).

Insistent PCs with a believable pretense can wrangle an appointment with Lydia. She also makes time for them if they come right out and say they're interested in spiral dust or missing homeless people. Lydia is pleasant and engaging, though she wears an oddly strong perfume (a PC who succeeds on a difficulty 3 Intellect-based task identifies it as insect repellent).

UTILITY

The utility closet has cleaning equipment, a hot water heater, electrical supply lines, and extra boxes of rock polish and metallic wire. It also contains a variety of tools, including several that could be used as medium weapons: a crowbar, an oversized wrench, and a couple of thick steel rods. Two high-power flashlights hang on the wall.

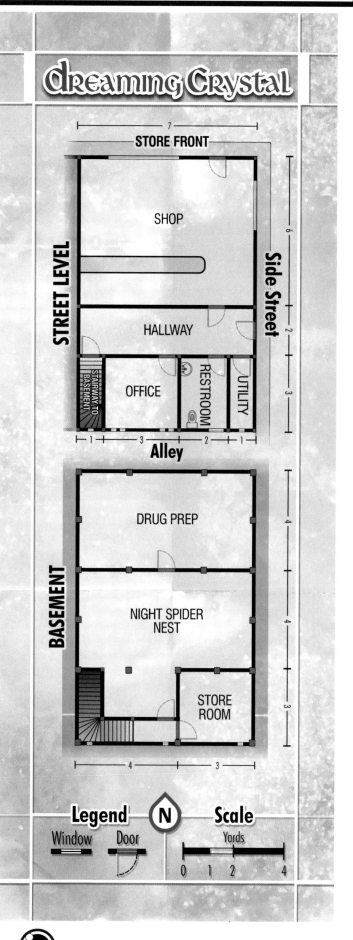

LYDIA TALKS ABOUT SPIRAL DUST

If the PCs ask Lydia Nance about spiral dust or missing homeless people, she realizes that her secret is blown, but she tries to salvage the situation.

Lydia tells the PCs that there's something they just *have* to see before she says anything else. Once they see it with their own eyes, then she'll talk. To say anything beforehand would just be wasted breath, she claims.

At this point, she gives the PCs the keys to the basement. She tells the characters to return to her office afterward, and then they can talk on equal footing about the real significance of spiral dust. If the PCs want her to accompany them to the basement, she is happy to either lead or follow.

If the characters take Lydia up on her deal, she expects that they will soon be dead. She intends to shoot any PCs who survive the night spider attack before they can leave the basement. If the PCs engage Lydia in combat, she fights to the death (or incapacity).

Lydia is not willing to divulge any information even under duress because she's terrified of Donna Ilsa. If the PCs come up with a way to make her talk, refer to the file called "Donna Ilsa" on her desktop computer, which sums up Lydia's knowledge and feelings on her involvement.

RESTROOM

This bathroom, used by staff and customers, is cleaned once a day by a service that shows up right before closing.

OFFICE

The Dreaming Crystal's business office is locked (with a level 5 mechanism) at all times, even when Lydia is inside.

The office features a desk cluttered with fossils and a desktop computer, filing cabinets, a safe, and a shelf filled with shipping supplies. A poster map of the world is stuck to one wall.

Internet Access: A Wi-Fi router sits beneath the desk. The Dreaming Crystal's network is called "Rocky Start" and the password is "chrysolite33," conveniently written on a sticky note next to the computer.

World Map: The map on the wall is of the whole Earth. Many blue pushpins are stuck in the map. If the PCs take the time, they count twenty pins almost (though not perfectly) equidistant from one another, such that the pins encompass the entire planet. One of the pins is stuck in Seattle, but most lie outside the borders of the USA and correspond with large cities (including Bangkok, Beijing, Buenos Aires, Cairo, Delphi, Istanbul, Karachi, Lagos, London, and so on). However, some pins don't correspond to any city visible at the scale the map allows, and a couple are pinned in the middle of the Atlantic or Pacific ocean.

Desktop Computer: Accessing the Wi-Fi is one thing, but logging onto the computer requires turning it on first; Lydia always turns it off when she's not using it, making a remote hack normally impossible. When the computer is on, bypassing the password is a difficulty 5 Intellect task.

The computer doesn't seem to get much use, but there are three items of note on the desktop: a folder named Spirals, a program called BTC Cryptocurrency Wallet, and a folder with a crow icon labeled Donna Ilsa. All three items are separately encrypted, and to access each one, a character must succeed on a separate difficulty 5 Intellect task.

Spirals Folder: If accessed, the Spirals folder contains twenty subfolders, each with a name, an address, and a paid balance of 10 to 20 units marked "BTC." One or more of the characters probably recognize BTC as Bitcoin and know that it's an alternative currency to regular money that's enjoyed some popularity in recent years.

The PCs might notice that the physical addresses in the Spirals folder correspond to the locations of the blue pins on the map. In fact, each pin represents a dealer (similar to LeRoy Cain) who receives spiral dust from Lydia. The list of names includes the following.

LeRoy Cain, Seattle
Obol Demer, Bangkok
Jack Chén, Beijing
Joaquin Lopez, Buenos Aires
Nader Boutros, Cairo
Sania Beti, Delphi
Elia Yilmaz, Istanbul

BTC Cryptocurrency Wallet: This program, if successfully accessed, is an electronic wallet that holds the sum of all the balances indicated in the Spirals folder (a total of 321 BTC). Characters can enrich themselves by stealing the cryptocurrency, but only if they've previously set up their own Bitcoin wallet and have a digital Bitcoin address to which to transfer the coins. Figuring out how to do that is as simple as spending about twenty minutes researching the topic on the Internet and downloading one of many suggested wallets.

Donna Ilsa Folder: The folder, marked with a crow icon, contains the photo of an ordinary-looking woman with black hair, dark eyes, and a hooked nose. Besides the image file, the folder contains a text document called Diary, which reads as follows.

"If I knew then what I know now, I'd have told Donna Ilsa that I wasn't interested. But I let greed rule me. And now those *things* live in my basement. If I don't continue preparing and shipping the dust to the list Ilsa supplied, they'll eat me, like the others. Or she'll come take care of me herself . . .

As long as I keep shipping out the spiral dust, I get to live. How did this happen?

And how does she deliver the raw product to the prep room every month without coming through the main shop? If she's trying to intimidate me with her ability to overcome any lock and evade all detection, she's succeeded. Sometimes I wonder if she isn't a demon, sent to torment me. I have nightmares about her. In them, her face peels away, revealing a crow's head with dead black eyes. It's horrifying.

If you're reading this, I'm probably dead. I deserve to die for the things I've done since Ilsa came. Don't be like me: stay away from spiral dust, stay away from my basement, and most of all, money can't buy back your safety once you've sold it."

Filing Cabinets: The filing cabinets are filled with legitimate material having to do with owning a rock shop, including contracts with suppliers, employee files, tax filings, deeds, records of sales going back at least ten years, and so on.

Safe: The safe is locked; cracking it is a difficulty 6 Intellect-based task. The safe contains about $2,000 in 20s and 50s, ten doses of spiral dust, and four cyphers: two level 5 stims and two level 4 meditation aids.

Shipping Supplies: In addition to collapsed cardboard boxes, foam popcorn, tape, and labels, the supplies include several cans of insect repellent.

BASEMENT

The door to the Dreaming Crystal's basement is kept locked (with a level 5 mechanism) at all times, even when Lydia is down below. The door is relatively sturdy, and breaking it down requires a successful difficulty 5 Might-based task. Lydia's key also opens it.

The stairs descend a couple of flights into a basement that's much deeper than standard. The hallway beyond the staircase's terminus opens onto a storeroom and a larger chamber where night spiders nest.

STOREROOM

The storeroom in the basement is filled with extra stock (geodes, postcards, lapidary supplies, receipt carbon paper, toilet paper, pens, and more—everything a functioning shop needs to have on hand for resupply). That includes a few more flashlights.

NIGHT SPIDER NEST

A "No Trespassing" sign is tacked on this heavy door, which is kept locked (with a level 6 mechanism) at all times, even when Lydia is inside. The door is exceptionally sturdy, and breaking it down requires a successful difficulty 6 Might-based task. Lydia's key also opens it.

A light switch just inside the door doesn't seem to work (though a water spigot beneath the switch issues a stream of water if turned on), so the room is dark. If Lydia is with the PCs, she gets some flashlights from the storeroom.

read aloud

Damp and warm, the air is stifling and smells vaguely of roadkill. Dozens of white plastic buckets filled to the brim with water are scattered across the cement floor. Hundreds of mosquitoes swarm over each bucket.

The buckets are filled with mosquito larvae, visible as thousands of tiny black dots swimming in the water. If the PCs walk into the room without any way of keeping the insects at bay, swarming mosquitoes bite so ferociously that the characters must succeed at a difficulty 2 Intellect defense roll each round or their actions are modified by one step to their detriment because of the distraction. (The question of why Lydia keeps so much insect repellent in her office is now answered.)

Stim, page 328

Meditation aid, page 322

Spiral Dust Effects

On Earth, a dose or hit of spiral dust comes in a tiny glass tube with a black screw-top cap; it looks very similar in other recursions. Several grains of blue dust (about a quarter of a gram) lie loose in the bottom of each tube. Users take a hit of spiral dust by letting a dose dissolve under the tongue or, for a more intense rush, by dropping the grains directly into their eyes for immediate absorption. The spiral dust produces its effects by inducing a temporary quickened-like status in users, even in creatures that are not quickened or do not possess the spark.

A hit of spiral dust translates as if it were a cypher, but it doesn't count against a PC's cypher limit. Most of the following effects are known by the Estate, and the PCs can get a report. The effects listed under Secret Effects are *not* initially known by the Estate, though the PCs likely discover them before the adventure's end.

Moderate User Effects: A dose of spiral dust has the following effects on a creature that doesn't often use the drug:

• Euphoria for one hour.

• The difficulty of all tasks related to noticing, perceiving, spotting clues, and seeing what's hidden decreases by three steps for one hour.

• The difficulty of all tasks related to combat increases by two steps for one hour.

Heavy User Effects: A dose has the effects described above, plus the following effects on creatures that regularly use the drug:

• Irises become purplish fractals (effect fades one month after last dose).

• User can see fully invisible objects and creatures and can see in the dark, through obscuring mist, and sometimes through walls for one hour after a dose.

• If a dose is taken before sleep, the user experiences intense dreams.

• Shaking hands and a difficult-to-deny urge to find more spiral dust occur if the user goes a day without a dose (effect fades one month after last dose).

Overdose Effects: An overdose has the effects described above, plus the following final effect on a creature that regularly uses the drug and finally takes too much:

• The user drops out, runs away, leaves her old life behind, and is never seen again.

Secret Effects: The special abilities gained from a drug dose stem from the user becoming partially quickened while the dose remains active.

Heavy User: The intense dreams of a heavy user represent the user's dream self appearing in a random recursion during the sleep period (the user's sleeping body does not go into abeyance). A naive user believes that the experience is only a vivid dream.

Overdose Effect: The user disappears because instead of her dream self appearing in a random recursion, she fully translates against her will and is deposited inside an entity called Nakarand, usually never to be seen again.

Dustman Effect: An entity known as the Dustman has a special connection to spiral dust and spiral dust users. See Intermission 1.

• Through a psychic connection, the Dustman can remotely control spiral dust addicts. When the Dustman lightly controls addicts, the victims are referred to as "partly activated" and can't remember anything that happened while they were so controlled.

• If the Dustman completely activates a spiral dust addict, the addict "dies" and a quickened zombie is born, intent on achieving the last command imparted by the Dustman.

Why Using Spiral Dust to Initiate a Translation Fails

Upon realizing that spiral dust comes from another recursion, clever PCs who understand the rules of translation might try to use a dose to initiate a translation and see where they end up. (An object from the destination recursion can normally be used to initiate translation.) However, this doesn't work for one simple reason—the ultimate source of spiral dust is Earth, which supplies Nakarand with the "raw material" that it converts into spiral dust.

Quickened, page 22

The spark, page 22

Abeyance, page 129

Nakarand, page 73

Intermission 1, page 23

Quickened zombie, page 25

The ceiling in this chamber is 25 feet (8 m) high and lost in darkness unless someone thinks to swing a light up to examine it. If the PCs direct their flashlights overhead, they see something much more disturbing than mosquitoes.

read aloud

Two spiders the size of horses cling to the high basement ceiling. Numerous bodies cocooned in grey webs hang unmoving around the eight-legged monsters.

The night spiders allow intruders into the room without drawing attention to themselves, but they attack as soon as anyone except Lydia tries to leave. The spiders were set to guard this "Earth distribution station" by Donna Ilsa, who also arranged for the mosquito farm. Despite the size mismatch, the thousands of breeding mosquitoes are sufficient to feed the spiders here, though just barely. One of Lydia's jobs is to maintain the mosquito farm and provide a higher-grade supplement every other week (which she culls from the homeless in nearby Boulder with promises of food and a place to sleep).

NIGHT SPIDER	4 (12)

Night spiders originate in Ardeyn's Night Vault, where the 5-foot (2 m) diameter adults (not including legs) nest along the Roads of Sorrow. Night spiders prefer to walk on floors and ceilings, and when they attach themselves to tunnel ceilings with webbing, their dangling legs can be mistaken for rootlets of the Daylands that have breached the vault.

Night spiders are particularly hardy if removed from their home recursion, which means that even if taken into a recursion (by inapposite gate or similar means) that doesn't operate under the law of Magic, their abilities don't see much degradation, especially if they hatched from eggs previously transferred to the new recursion.

Motive: Hungers for flesh

Environment (Ardeyn | Magic): Underground areas in groups of one to six

Health: 16

Damage Inflicted: 4 points

Movement: Short

Modifications: Attacks as level 5; perception as level 6; Speed defense as level 3 due to size.

Combat: A night spider can bite a foe with its mandibles but prefers to use web strands to attack a target within short range. The

Show 'Em: Night Spiders, Image E, page 93

webbing inflicts no damage but is amazingly sticky. A webbed character who fails a Might defense roll is dragged within immediate range of the spider (possibly hoisted up into the air if the night spider is attached to a wall or ceiling). The night spider attacks only one foe at a time, and only creatures of about human size or smaller.

Breaking free from a web strand is a level 4 Might-based task. A strand can also be severed if it takes 8 points of damage.

Victims unable to break free from the web are automatically cocooned one round after being dragged into immediate range by the spider's spare legs, which hold a victim immobile (allowing only purely mental actions or escape attempts). Each round the victim remains cocooned, he automatically takes 4 points of ambient damage from suffocation. Breaking free from a cocoon is a difficulty 6 Might-based task, and a cocoon can be opened if it takes 25 points of damage.

If a night spider is killed, a mass of tiny spiderling eggs in its internal cavity convulsively hatch. Spiderlings rush out in an unstoppable swarm, and before they disperse, they inflict 4 points of damage to all creatures in immediate range who fail a Speed defense roll.

Interaction: A guard colony of night spiders can sometimes be established if a handful of eggs are transplanted to an area before they hatch. Adult night spiders are not particularly discriminating in their prey, but they can be trained to ignore certain individuals.

Use: A clutch of night spiders guards the vault of a recursor on Earth that the PCs have reason to investigate.

Loot: The bodies of cocooned night spider victims have normal gear for the recursion in which they're found, which sometimes includes a cypher.

Victims on Ceiling: If the PCs defeat the spiders, they can investigate the many cocooned, blood-drained, and somewhat mummified remains of previous victims. The victims include a couple of college kids who broke into the shop on a lark and made it into the basement, a thief who broke into the shop and thought she'd found the mother lode, and about eight homeless people Lydia lured from the streets of Boulder to supplement the night spiders' mosquito diet.

Nothing of much value persists on the corpses, though the PCs can identify the college kids by their IDs (Maya Haskins and George Parks, whose disappearance a few months ago in Boulder created a media firestorm, though that's mostly blown over by the time the characters discover the truth).

DRUG PREP

read aloud

Yellow packing tape marks out an empty space on the floor of this room that's roughly square, about 6 feet (2 m) to a side. Written in large black marker on the tape is the warning "Stand Clear." Racks of tiny glass bottles with black screw caps, all empty, line two walls. A work bench opposite the taped-off floor space is cluttered with funnels, loose glass bottles, boxes of nylon gloves, a few pairs of safety goggles, respirators, and a couple of fine bristle brushes.

Close examination of the work bench reveals tiny particles of spiral dust scattered about, but hardly enough for a single dose. The glass bottles are empty, waiting to be filled with doses. Beneath the work bench stored on a shelf is a wide plastic tray with high edges and a couple of ball peen hammers (the bin and hammers are also contaminated with spiral dust).

What's Going On: Donna Ilsa, Lydia's taskmaster and source for spiral dust, lives in an alternate recursion known as Crow Hollow. Once every few weeks, she translates into the room (appearing in the taped-off area) carrying solid "bricks" of spiral dust, leaves the bricks, and translates back to her home recursion. (Spiral dust can translate along with a recursor because of its special nature.) Lydia never sees Donna Ilsa arrive because of Ilsa's late schedule; she just knows that every so often, the latest delivery appears in the taped-off section of the prep room.

Lydia takes the bricks (which are more like pieces of rubble from broken statuary), batters them to dust, fills glass bottles, and caps them to create individual doses. Then she carries the lot up to her office, prepares them for shipping to dealers across the globe, and mails them out with the other merchandise.

NEXT STEPS FOR THE PCs

After the PCs wrap up their business at the Dreaming Crystal rock shop (and possibly take

Lydia out of the picture), they might want to return to the Estate to report back or conduct research. The GM can suggest this if the PCs don't think of it themselves. At the very least, reporting back to Lawrence Keaton is probably advisable.

Whether through their own research or from Keaton after they report in, the PCs learn the following:

• A recursor by the name of Donna Ilsa is noted in the Estate database.

• Donna Ilsa is a member of the Beak Mafia, though her place in the hierarchy isn't known.

• The Estate doesn't have any operatives in Crow Hollow, where the Beak Mafia operates, but they do have an object brought to Earth through an inapposite gate that can serve as the seed of a translation: a black feather (a kro's feather, though very crowlike to be sure).

• The PCs can learn the general information that all recursors know about Crow Hollow, as described in the corebook, as well as the name of the head of the largest Beak Mafia family: Don Wyclef.

• PCs who try to use spiral dust to initiate a translation just to see where they end up fail to go anywhere, as described under "Spiral Dust Effects."

Optional: Sometime during this transition period, the events of Intermission 1 (page 23) could occur.

Upon piecing the clues together, the PCs could also decide to wait in the rock shop's drug prep room until the next shipment of spiral dust arrives. If they pursue this path, Donna Ilsa translates into the taped-off square with another raw spiral dust chunk in 1d6 + 6 days. See "Confronting Donna Ilsa" in the next chapter for her stats and her reaction to the PCs. She always translates with two additional night spiders (adults) for protection. Rather than fight, she attempts to flee using a cypher she keeps handy for that purpose.

CROW HOLLOW

The recursion of Crow Hollow is hosted in the branches of a massive tree. It's most known for its Glittering Market, an always-open bazaar whose fascinating and hard-to-find goods are collected from many recursions. Items both wondrous and mundane can be had in the market, including objects taken from nearly any recursion created by fictional leakage one might care to name. If it wasn't for the Beak Mafia constantly shaking down shop-owners for protection money, the place would be an idyllic consumer wonderland.

Show 'Em: *Glittering Market, Image F, page 93*

Confronting Donna Ilsa, page 45

Crow Hollow, page 242

Spiral Dust Effects, page 36

The Beak Mafia is Crow Hollow's surprisingly large underworld. Despite outward appearances of solidarity, several kro crime families make up the mafia. Some of the families are allied with each other, while others are bitter rivals.

MAFIA GANG WARFARE

The current head of the largest Beak Mafia family is Wyclef Drood, or as most call him, Don Wyclef. He employs a flock of muscle kro to collect protection money and patrol against the common thievery and the inroads made by rival kro crime families. Drood's largest rival is the Cornaro family, led by Donna Ilsa Cornaro.

The rivalry has grown so pronounced that violence has spilled into the market, affecting business. That's not good for anybody. Both Donna Ilsa and Don Wyclef want the gang war to end, but both want to win that war, so neither is backing down. Both have gone to extraordinary lengths to defeat the other, including calling on aid from powers beyond the recursion of Crow Hollow.

TRANSLATING TO CROW HOLLOW

PCs can use their type abilities to translate to Crow Hollow. If any PC has previously traveled to the recursion, that person can initiate the translation. If no one has previously visited, the PCs need another option. As it happens, the Estate's Gate House keeps items taken via inapposite travel from various recursions, and in the case of Crow Hollow, that item is a black kro feather. The PCs can use the feather (this is the route Keaton suggests, though he cautions them to leave the feather behind when they go) or find some other way to get to Crow Hollow.

When the PCs translate, the process imprints on them the tidbits of knowledge that a recursor knows about Crow Hollow, if they didn't already research that information in the Estate library. The characters can also choose to become kro to better fit into the context of the recursion.

Arriving in Crow Hollow via Translation: The default location for first-time translators is right in the middle of the Glittering Market. A PC who has previously visited and initiated the translation appears with her group wherever she last left.

Glittering Market: This multilevel bazaar is built in the branches of a massive tree. Gaudy and spectacular, the shop stalls compete to draw the eye of potential buyers, and flashing, magical firefly lights are a popular tactic. The market is composed primarily of kro, and few kro ever saw a gaudy piece of clothing or costume accessory they didn't like. Thus, customers and shopkeepers alike are dressed in fashions nearly as startling as the many odd items for sale in the market.

Racial Makeup of Crow Hollow: It's immediately obvious that most of the people in Crow Hollow look like humanoid crows. They wear clothing, use tools, and speak a language much like English, but they have beaks instead of mouths and feathers instead of hair. Though kro predominate, much of the merchandise here is shipped in through the Strange, which means that a sizeable number of people in Crow Hollow are human (because when one enters a recursion via direct interface with the Strange, it's like traveling through an inapposite gate). A smattering of qephilim and other, stranger races native

What a Recursor Knows About Crow Hollow, page 243

Security of a Beak Mafia Home, page 44

The Dustman Arrives, page 79

KEEPING THE ADVENTURE ON TRACK

The portion of the adventure that occurs in Crow Hollow eventually provides the PCs with a route for learning the location of the spiral dust factory (if they agree to help Donna Ilsa recover her stolen eggs). If the PCs move forward on that track, job done.

However, if they strike out on their own and don't go after the eggs, they'll have to come up with another way of gaining the information they need. One option might be to find the mafia supplier themselves.

It's easy for the PCs to trace the teams of kro goons on their daily routes. It's less easy to know when a particular group is carrying a brick of spiral dust to one of the dealers in the Glittering Market. And it's fiendishly difficult to witness the arrival of spiral dust *within* a secure chamber inside the Drood or Cornaro homes. Still, the PCs might devise a plan that allows them to infiltrate one of the drug-dealing Beak Mafia families, despite the stiff challenges described in "Security of a Beak Mafia Home."

PCs who manage to infiltrate a home eventually witness the Dustman when he appears, and they can directly interact with him. This scenario is unlikely, but if it happens, see "The Dustman Arrives."

to recursions in the Shoals of Earth are also represented.

SHOPPING IN CROW HOLLOW

Characters on a shopping trip can find many strange and wonderful things in the Glittering Market, such as magic charms, fabulous clothing, weapons and valuables from other recursions (and Earth), and, if they look hard enough, even a few cyphers and hits of spiral dust, though at incredibly jacked-up prices.

Crow Coin: All prices are paid in crow coin (CC), which characters might discover the truth about upon their first purchase. After a contractual handshake sealing the deal, the shop owner pulls her hand back with the agreed-upon amount of crow coin glittering in her taloned palm, and the same number of points debited from the PC as damage.

If PCs are looking for something particular but mundane, they find it after searching the stalls for 1d6 +2 × 30 minutes. If searching for something a bit more outre (such as a cypher, an artifact, or spiral dust), they must spend the indicated time searching and succeed on a difficulty 3 Intellect-based task.

Regardless of the results, the PCs also find one of the following items. Each item is one of a kind, unless noted otherwise. Some are essentially minor artifacts, others little more than frippery.

1. Globe filled with tiny, glowing, flying humanoids that provides light as bright as a flashlight; 2 CC (Magic)
2. Powdered pet; add water to create a level 3 dog similar to a pit bull; some training required; 3 CC (Mad Science)
3. Shotgun shells packed with depleted uranium (8 points of damage per shell); 5 CC per shell (Standard Physics)
4. Red cloak that reduces older user to age 10 while wearing it; depletion 1 in 1d20; 10 CC (Magic)
5. A violin purporting to be a Stradivarius; 200 CC (Standard Physics)
6. A chest of soil and writhing worms, guaranteed to eat anything placed inside; depletion 1 in 1d20; 15 CC (Mad Science)
7. Reversible set of clothing: elegant dress on one side, light-eating black bodysuit on the other; 8 CC (Magic)
8. 100 days of nutrition and hydration in tiny pill form; 5 CC (Mad Science)

Crow coin, page 243

If any of the PCs aren't at their cypher limit, the market is a great place to "top off" if they have time to shop.

ILLUMINATED GLOBE.
BRIGHT AS A FLASHLIGHT — NO NEED FOR BATTERIES

DEPLETED URANIUM SHELLS.
WHEN BLOWING SOMETHING TO PIECES JUST ISN'T ENOUGH!

ERADICATING WORMS.
GUARANTEED TO REMOVE ALL TRACES

SUPERCYCLE.
VRRRROOOOOOOOM!!!!

BRAIN BUD GRAFT.
UNLOCK YOUR FULL POTENTIAL! PET PACKAGE

SPORE WORM URINE VAPORIZER.
REPELS 94% OF SPORE WORM SPECIES!

POWDERED PET.
DANGER
JUST ADD WATER

DRAGON HORN.
DRACONIS VOCARE

*Asking about the spiral
dust trade gets the PCs
noticed by more than
just the Beak Mafia.
Word also gets back
to the Dustman, and
then to Uentaru (if she
hasn't heard already),
which sets in motion
the events described
in Intermission 1 on
page 23.*

GM Intrusion: *The kro
goon employs a clever
trick with a wave of
its black wings, and
instead of the character
successfully attacking
the kro goon, the PC
successfully attacks a
nearby ally or innocent
bystander instead.*

9	A happy mask that changes the user's mood to happy when worn; depletion 1 in 1d20; 10 CC (Magic)
10	Cypher: sniper module; 10 CC
11	Stuffed flying monkey, posed to pounce, a bit worn; 10 CC (Any)
12	Latest smartphone with SIM card (limited functionality away from Earth); 8 CC (Standard Physics)
13	Dragon horn; attracts the attention of the closest dragon for miles around in recursions inhabited by dragons; 20 CC (Magic)
14	Extra arm graft; performs all activities of a normal arm but the difficulty of actions is modified by two steps to the user's detriment; 12 CC (Mad Science)
15	Brain bud graft; once per day, an Intellect action taken by the user is one step less difficult, but the user is inflicted with a Tourette-like syndrome that makes all interaction-related tasks two steps more difficult (and similar tasks for allies are one step more difficult when the user is near); 8 CC (Mad Science)
16	A rod that fires an amazing ray of color and light that bursts like fireworks overhead; depletion 1 in 1d20; 10 CC (Magic)
17	Cypher: speed boost; 10 CC
18	Gauntlet with a mechanical suction device on the palm that serves as an asset for all tasks related to climbing and gripping; depletion 1 in 1d100; 5 CC (Standard Physics)
19	Spore worm urine vaporizer; repels spore worms of Ruk for one minute when sprayed; depletion 1–2 in 1d20; 5 CC (Mad Science)
20	Motorcycle (a fictional leakage version of a Tomahawk V10 Superbike) with 10 gallons of gasoline (0 to 60 in 2.5 seconds, with a top speed above 300 mph); 500 CC (Standard Physics)

FINDING A SPIRAL DUST DEALER

If the PCs search the Glittering Market and find a spiral dust dealer, that dealer is a shopkeeper whose primary wares are something else entirely (tea, coffee, tobacco, spirits, and so on). On the topic of spiral dust, all the dealers are extraordinarily tight-lipped and share only the following information.

• They confirm that they sell spiral dust.
• The price is 12 CC per hit. Most dealers have at most five hits for sale at any one time.

• Only two families are behind the spiral dust trade in Crow Hollow: the Drood family, led by Don Wyclef, and the Cornaro family, led by Donna Ilsa.

• They indicate whether their supplier is the Drood family or the Cornaro family (it's about 50-50 for a randomly discovered dealer).

• Don Wyclef can't be reasoned or bargained with, and anyone who tries to work out a deal will soon be dead for their trouble. Negotiating is safe only if Don Wyclef comes looking for a deal; otherwise, approaching him is as good as asking for a bullet to the brain.

If the PCs become too disruptive, they attract the attention of several kro goons in the employ of Don Wyclef who actually *do* provide protection services, especially to dealers of spiral dust (in case the rival gang tries to put them out of business). See below for kro goon stats.

FINDING THE BEAK MAFIA

PCs can find representatives of the Beak Mafia without too much trouble. Shaking down a drug dealer in the Glittering Market is one way (mafia kro goons respond to such intrusive activities). Asking nearly any shop owner who they pay protection money to is another. With enough wheedling or bribes, or after making a sale, the PCs can learn where to find the Drood family house or the Cornaro family roost.

A third way of making contact with the Beak Mafia is by becoming involved in random gang violence through a group GM intrusion.

KRO GOON   4 (12)

Some kro have no compunction about taking crow coin for any job under the sun—the more violent and less thought required, the better. These toughs always find a Beak Mafia family ready to accept them with open wings. New recruits are trained in a brutal lost-world recursion that eats normal wise kro for breakfast. Survivors are slapped with the label "kro goon" and become part of whichever family sponsored them.

Motive: Getting paid for violent or shady activities

Environment (Crow Hollow | Magic, Mad Science): Anywhere, usually in groups of five to ten

Health: 12

Damage Inflicted: 4 points

Armor: 1

Movement: Short when walking or gliding

Modifications: Perception as level 6; all tasks related to seeing through duplicity or disguises as level 6.

Combat: Some kro goons have medium pistols that can target a foe within long range. Other kro goons have longer-barreled medium rifles able to spray bullets at up to four targets within short range as a single action (but the difficulty of such attacks is increased by one step, and each time a kro goon sprays bullets, it must spend its next turn reloading its gun).

One in five kro goons has an artifact weapon that operates under the law of Magic or the law of Mad Science:

Typical Magic Artifact: A staff that fires lightning bolts at one target within long range for 6 points of damage. Depletion: 1 in 1d20.

Typical Mad Science Artifact: A mini rocket launcher able to fire a missile at a target the user can see within a half mile. The missile explodes on impact, dealing 4 points of ambient damage to all creatures in immediate range who fail a Speed defense roll (and 1 point to those who succeed). Depletion: 1–2 in 1d6.

Kro can fall safely from any height and can glide five times as far as the distance fallen (or much farther, if one is skilled in gliding and the use of thermals).

Interaction: Kro goons trust their compatriots and their family, though most will at least listen to a pitch describing the superior benefits and pay they would receive by taking coin from a competing interest.

Use: When a Beak Mafia family wants something done, it sends a crew of kro goons.

Loot: In addition to the weapons described under Combat, a kro goon is about 20% likely to carry one random cypher. Each kro goon also carries 3d6 crow coins.

DROOD FAMILY HOUSE

The Drood family house, under the control of Don Wyclef, is located a few levels down from the main market levels. PCs can find it by asking around and getting directions, by paying someone to lead them to it, or perhaps after being captured by kro goons in a run-in.

read aloud

It's difficult to tell where this elaborate structure ends and the tree of Crow Hollow begins because a portion of it is carved into the trunk itself. The only obvious entrance is behind two massive, shiny metallic doors set back from a wide, pillared porch. Kro goons guard the house: some on the porch, several on slender turrets arranged at strategic points around the building, and a few in the lane leading up to the house.

Typical kro shopkeeper: level 2

Don Wyclef, page 243

Approaching Don Wyclef: *Every NPC (including kro goons) who overhears the PCs discussing the idea of talking with the Drood family or Don Wyclef warns them not to do it. Don Wyclef is a known quantity. He doesn't make deals; he just rolls over opposition. And he especially hates outsiders.*

Elite kro goon: level 6; health 18; Armor 2; attacks two targets in long range with a pistol as a single action, dealing 6 points of damage per shot

Edward McCreary: level 5, level 6 for all tasks related to duplicity

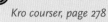

Kro courser, page 278

Kro goon, page 42

Night spider, page 37

A total of fifteen kro goons guard the exterior of the house, and as many as ten elite kro goons are on hand to provide additional backup. Other powerful Drood assets are available if the PCs try a frontal assault. Talking is only slightly more fruitful.

Talking With the Drood Family: If the characters tell the door guards that they have information about the spiral dust business being run by Donna Ilsa Cornaro (or if they come up with another equally compelling reason), they're told that they'll be killed if they insist on seeing someone in the family. Don Wyclef hates outsiders. But PCs who persist can get a conference with Edward McCreary, Wyclef's chief lieutenant.

Refreshments in the Salon: If the PCs talk their way into the house, they are ushered just inside the main front doors into a large salon (hardwood floor, no windows, gilt wallpaper, big table) where refreshments are served (crackers and cheese). At least ten kro goons from the outside accompany the PCs into the house to keep an eye on them.

Drood Representative: Eventually, a kro dressed in dapper clothing appears, walking with a cane. He introduces himself as Edward McCreary and says he handles business for Don Wyclef. McCreary speaks with an English accent and blinks nonstop. Nearly everything he tells the characters is a lie.

In a nutshell, McCreary intends to pump the PCs for information, then have them killed by the ten kro goons in the room. If he can manage it, McCreary avoids monologuing in case the PCs survive the encounter.

Right up until the moment he orders their deaths, McCreary reassures the PCs that they made the right decision coming to see Don Wyclef, and that he's certain they can work something out as long as the characters tell him everything. But once that's settled, he orders the goons to tear off the PCs' heads and arms (or wings, if they became kro upon translating).

Fighting Free of the Salon: To fight their way out of the Drood house, the PCs first have to defeat (or get away from) the ten kro goons in the salon, and then do the same for the guards remaining outside the house.

CORNARO FAMILY ROOST

The Cornaro family roost, under the control of Donna Ilsa, is located several levels above the main market levels. PCs who go looking for the roost can find it by asking around and

---

SECURITY OF A BEAK MAFIA HOME

It's devilishly difficult to infiltrate a Beak Mafia house under false pretenses, given that kro goons are on guard specifically to prevent such an intrusion. Goons are suspicious of everyone, and even if a PC impersonates a fellow guard, she must come up with the correct phrases for passing between secure areas, which are also usually locked (with a level 5 or 6 mechanism).

The outside of a mafia house has about ten to fifteen kro goons on watch at any one time. If the PCs decide (against all good sense) to penetrate farther *into* a Beak Mafia house, two or three elite kro goons show up if an alarm is raised, in addition to a dozen more regular goons. If you need to come up with a floor plan for such an undertaking, an Internet search for "mansion floor plan" provides several options you can adapt to the PCs' (possibly suicidal) desires.

---

getting directions, by paying someone to lead them to it, or perhaps by tailing Donna Ilsa after she translates back from Earth.

read aloud

Massive iron cables bolted to the bottom of one of Crow Hollow's gargantuan branches suspend an elaborate tree house over empty blue sky and white clouds. A spiral staircase winds down one iron cable, allowing visitors to descend to the roofwide balcony that also serves as the main entrance of the roost. In addition to tasteful rooftop landscaping that includes potted plants, benches, and comfortable lounge chairs, the top level hosts patrolling kro goons and a few "pet" kro coursers that apparently have the run of the place.

A total of ten kro goons and two trained kro coursers guard the exterior of the roost. If the PCs try to force their way in, up to ten elite kro goons appear within a few rounds to provide additional backup. The PCs are better off staying on the balcony level and trying to talk their way into a meeting with Donna Ilsa. Otherwise, the roost has the typical security of a Beak Mafia home. In addition, Donna Ilsa enjoys the protection of several night spiders trained to ignore the members of her household.

Talking With the Cornaro Family: PCs looking for a face-to-face meeting with Donna Ilsa can get one if they tell the door guards that they have information about the spiral dust business she runs on Earth (or if they come up with another equally compelling reason).

Rooftop Gazebo Meeting: If the PCs succeed on a bid to talk with someone in the Cornaro roost, they're ushered to a large gazebo on the balcony. The gazebo is securely locked from the outside before Donna Ilsa enters through a second entrance in the gazebo floor.

In addition to three elite kro goons inside the gazebo, the tall gazebo roof hosts a night spider nest and two night spiders. The spiders watch the PCs avidly with their many eyes, quivering in their eagerness to attack any characters who show the slightest sign of hostility or even move too quickly.

If the PCs previously dealt with Ilsa and things got off to a bad start in that first meeting, she still might be willing to talk to them now because she wants something from them.

CONFRONTING DONNA ILSA

Donna Ilsa usually wears dark, elegant dresses, fine pearls, and designer sunglasses, even when inside. Several gaudy rings cover the fingers emerging from her feathered wings, but despite her accoutrements, she comports herself as one constantly struggling to escape from stifling depression. She's the opposite of cheery and can't see the humor in anything.

Donna Ilsa's Motivations: Ilsa's motives are complicated, but they boil down to a toxic mixture of despair, regret, and vindictiveness. She despairs that she'll never see her kidnapped offspring (in egg form) again, she regrets that she got into the spiral dust trade to raise funds to locate her eggs, but she vindictively refuses to back down from that trade now that Don Wyclef is trying to take it from her. She can't stomach another loss. The only way she can see through her current situation is if she can get her eggs back. The quickened, nonaligned PCs are the first glimmer of hope she's seen in a long time.

Ilsa Makes A Deal: Donna Ilsa relates the following information during regular conversation. (Summary: She promises to tell the PCs where to find the factory that makes

spiral dust if they rescue her kidnapped eggs.) She never lies to the characters, though she does not reveal answers until the PCs deliver on their end of any bargain that's struck.

• "I won't tell you who my raw spiral dust supplier is . . . unless we reach an understanding. I'm at my wing's end. I need resolution, and maybe, just maybe . . . we can help each other."

• "I expanded the spiral dust trade I started here in Crow Hollow to Earth. My supplier suggested it as a way to one-up Don Wyclef. He even provided me with a list of dealers to use on Earth." (LeRoy Cain was one of those supplied names, which Donna Ilsa passed on to Lydia Nance.)

• "Someone kidnapped my five precious eggs a year ago. I haven't been able to find out who, or why. In my desperation, I made a deal with a spiral dust supplier who'd approached me only days earlier. I'd rebuffed him once before, but I agreed after my eggs went missing. I needed the extra funds from the dust sales to do whatever it took to get my eggs back."

• "Apparently, Wyclef made a similar deal. He set up his own spiral dust operation in Crow Hollow and would've cut me out completely if I had done nothing. Instead of focusing on retrieving my eggs, I spend my days beating back Don Wyclef's advances. This isn't what I wanted, but I'm locked down. I want my eggs, but by the Great Claw, I won't give up Crow Hollow to Don Wyclef without a fight."

• "While the war rages, I can't afford to spend the resources I sought to gain by dealing spiral dust. But I've finally learned where my eggs are being held. If *you* retrieve them, I'll give you the information you want."

• "I don't care if you destroy the spiral dust source because that means Wyclef will also be out of business. Crow Hollow can go back to the way it was before all this madness began."

Kro eggs are about the size of grapefruits, blue with black speckles, and remain essentially viable for years before they are brooded by their mother or father.

Donna Ilsa: level 7; health 24; Armor 2; attacks two targets in long range with a pistol as a single action, dealing 7 points of damage per shot; carries a level 5 anoetic grenade (recursion) whose endpoint is set for the center of the Glittering Market in Crow Hollow

Intermission 1: *If
the PCs return to the
Estate after accepting
Donna Ilsa's proposal
or at any point while
attempting to retrieve
the eggs from the
Mouth of Swords, they
might encounter the
events of Intermission 1
(page 23).*

Mouth of Swords

OVERLAND MAP

Ibora Forest

Path of the Dead

Tyvium River

Citadel Hazurrium

Zwya River

Trade Road

Old Road

Faustin

Hawran Mere

Little Baz

Emirzel Keep

Khaibur Woods

Gambrion Cliffs

Mouth of Swords

N

Legend:
- Capital City
- Town
- Dungeon

100 Miles

*Whole Body Grafts,
page 65*

**Experience Point
Awards:** *A PC gains 1
XP if she purchases one
or more items from the
Glittering Market. The
PCs gain 2 XP each if
they make a deal with
Donna Ilsa to find her
eggs, and another 2 XP
each if they learn the
location of the spiral
dust factory in Ruk
(regardless of whether
they return her eggs).
This is in addition to
any XP earned by other
means.*

Next Steps: If the PCs agree to Donna Ilsa's
proposal, she provides them with a rough,
tattered map to a location in the recursion
of Ardeyn called the Mouth of Swords.
According to the map, the Mouth of Swords
is located some 75 miles (121 km) south of
Citadel Hazurrium, near the tip of a ridge line
called the Gambrion Cliffs. (The PCs should

memorize the map before they translate to
Ardeyn because it won't go with them under
normal circumstances.)

Ilsa knows precious little about the Mouth
of Swords other than its location and the fact
that her kidnapped eggs are there. If the PCs
ask how she knows her eggs are there, she
sighs disconsolately and says only, "A cypher
told my fortune."

Finally, Donna Ilsa offers the PCs the
following three unique cyphers as down
payment on their services:

• A level 5 anoetic force screen projector that
creates an immobile plane of solid force up to
20 feet by 20 feet (6 m by 6 m) for one hour.
The screen can be tuned to be transparent,
be opaque, or act like a telephoto lens with
50x zoom. The plane conforms to the space
available.

• A level 4 anoetic friction-reducing gel
that creates an area of slipperiness within
short range. For one hour, the difficulty of
movement tasks in an immediate area is
increased by three steps. If a creature falls in
the area covered by the gel, it must make a
Might defense roll or be knocked unconscious
by fumes for one minute.

• A level 6 occultic psychic communique
that allows the user to project a one-time
telepathic message to anyone she knows with
unlimited range in any recursion (or on Earth).
Upon receiving the message, the recipient can
choose to respond. Each message can be up
to thirty-three words.

RETURNING DONNA ILSA'S EGGS

If the PCs return some or all of Ilsa's stolen
eggs, they make a friend for life—if they want
a friend who heads up a Beak Mafia family.
She keeps her word and gives up her supplier
(the Dustman) and the location she visited
once in the recursion of Ruk: a biomod shop
in Harmonious called Whole Body Grafts.

If the PCs reveal to Donna Ilsa that it was
very likely the Dustman who stole her eggs
in the first place, they witness something of
a nervous breakdown alternating between
terrifying rage and uncontrollable weeping. It's
something she worried about in her darkest
moments but didn't really believe. At any
rate, if the PCs go on to stop the flow of spiral
dust into Crow Hollow, Donna Ilsa accepts it,
though Don Wyclef is less understanding, and
the PCs should hope he never learns who cut
into his action.

MOUTH OF SWORDS

This adventure is part of the main arc of The Dark Spiral *and is appropriate for PCs who met Donna Ilsa in Crow Hollow and agreed to rescue her kidnapped eggs. As a stand-alone scenario, "Mouth of Swords" is a great "classic" adventure featuring exploration, puzzles, fearsome creatures of Ardeyn, and the possibility of garnering potent treasures. In either case, it gives the PCs a chance to enjoy the fantastic aspects of Ardeyn.*

BACKGROUND

Ardeyn operates under the law of Magic and is host to innumerable magical creatures and NPCs, including powerful undead spirits called wrath lords. A wrath lord named Myth Keeper established an arcane depository where other creatures and individuals of Ardeyn sometimes store valuables of various kinds. A year ago, a Stranger calling himself the Dustman brought several kro eggs (stolen from Donna Ilsa) to be stored in the Mouth of Swords. That's where they've remained ever since.

SYNOPSIS

PCs who investigate the Mouth of Swords encounter the wrath lord named Myth Keeper and its magical depository. They also likely learn that merely killing the wrath lord once isn't enough—they must track down and destroy its secret life, too. If the characters have come for Donna Ilsa's kidnapped eggs, they also discover that the eggs are not kept in a single handy location, but rather spread through multiple vaults. But if the PCs persevere, they can acquire every missing egg. (The same is true if the characters came to the Mouth of Swords seeking some other item of value.)

GETTING THE PCs INVOLVED

If the PCs are Estate operatives, the most straightforward way to bring them into this part of the adventure is by having Donna Ilsa recruit them in the previous chapter. If that doesn't work out, try the following option.

Non-Estate PCs: The head of the Cornaro family doesn't care who she contracts--- PCs with any affiliation (or none) draw her attention. Donna Ilsa has a problem: her unhatched eggs have been stolen by rival mafioso Don Wyclef. Donna offers the PCs two chests of crow coin if they safely return her eggs without alerting Wyclef that they are working for her.

Alternatively, PCs adventuring across Ardeyn discover a treasure map pointing out the Mouth of Swords south of Citadel Hazurrium. Written in the margin are the words "Treasures of magic and gold, guaranteed safe while on deposit. Inquire after Myth Keeper."

MODIFYING FOR DIFFERENT TIERS

For each tier that the characters' average tier is above 2, add two more spirits of wrath and one more sark to encounters that contain those creatures.

If the PCs are third tier or higher, increase the level of all creatures encountered by 3. See Modifying a Creature's Level for additional guidance.

ARDEYN

The Mouth of Swords lies in the recursion of Ardeyn, so the PCs must translate there. Ardeyn is a wide land that hosts sorcerers, dragons, magic swords, and sleeping gods, a grand fantasy that grew out of Sumerian myths, not medieval European ones. *The Strange* corebook has a complete summary of the recursion.

TRANSLATING TO ARDEYN

PCs can use their type abilities to translate to Ardeyn. If any PC has previously traveled to the recursion, that character can initiate the translation. If no one has previously visited, PCs working for the Estate received special training that includes knowledge of three specific, related pieces of information about Ardeyn, which provide the impetus for the translation trance. Alternatively, the PCs might find another way to get to the recursion.

When the PCs translate, the process

Wrath lord, page 52

Myth keeper, page 51

Modifying a Creature's Level, page 16

Ardeyn, page 160

imprints on them the tidbits of knowledge that a recursor knows about Ardeyn, if they didn't already know those things thanks to their training. The characters can choose to keep a human form or become qephilim.

Arriving in Ardeyn via Translation: The default location for first-time translators to Ardeyn is standing before the gates of Citadel Hazurrium in the Queendom. A PC who has previously visited and initiated the translation appears with his group wherever he last left.

Gates of Hazurrium: This immense fortress sports equally immense gates, made of two great valves of magically reinforced bronze. The gates, usually open by day, are overlooked by guard balconies and yet higher levels and balconies that climb the amazingly tall sides of Hazurrium. Through the open gates, a visitor can spy a many-storied interior composed of tree-lined streets, verandas and porches thick with hanging vegetation, spiraling stairs and catwalks, and brilliantly lit homes.

TRAVELING ACROSS ARDEYN
Approximately 75 miles (121 km) separate Hazurrium from the Mouth of Swords (see the overland map on page 46). Unpaved trade paths connect small villages and tiny keeps for most of the way, but the overland trip still requires at least three or four days of travel on foot (half that if the PCs acquire mounts in Hazurrium). During this trip, the characters might pass small villages (including Faustin)

and a few small keeps (including Emirzel), and they might have several chances for random encounters.

Faustin: This village is large enough to host a small inn called the Wings where travelers stay and locals gather for a drink in the evening. The proprietor is a thin man named Tarnic who dislikes the adventurers who sometimes operate out of Hazurrium.

Emirzel Keep: Baronet Emirzel was once a peacemaker pledged to the Queendom, but for her bravery in the line of duty, she was granted a small keep in the hinterlands. Emirzel is a human woman in her 50s, but she is quite hale and has half a mind to accompany any adventurers (as opposed to the usual traders or farmers) she finds on the road. At the very least, she puts up the PCs in her cramped keep.

Random Road Encounters: Each day the PCs travel between Hazurrium and the Mouth of Swords, they might have a random encounter, if you wish. Not all encounters necessarily lead to combat. For every tier the characters are above 1, add another creature of the same type as those encountered.

1–2	1d6 marauding sark
3–4	1d6 + 6 bandits (criminals)
5	4 Free Battalion qephilim mercenaries
6	3 rogue qephilim umber judges

MOUTH OF SWORDS

The PCs can try to learn more about the Mouth of Swords by asking around in Hazurrium or the small villages they pass as they travel toward the point on the map Donna Ilsa showed them. A PC who translated to Ardeyn might also have access to the Ardeyn lore skill.

Most Ardeyn natives don't know much about the Mouth of Swords, but characters can glean the following rumors of the place with persistence (or a successful difficulty 3 Intellect-based roll for someone with Ardeyn lore; one roll per rumor):

• The Mouth of Swords is an ancient qephilim burial place.

• A crazed spirit of wrath guards the Mouth of Swords, as do many lesser spirits, traps, and sorcerous wards.

• Treasures from the Age of Myth are kept in the Mouth of Swords, and they have lured more than one adventuring company to its doom.

• Those who have something they want to keep safe will find no better vault than that which lies behind the Mouth of Swords.

In addition, a PC who asks around the villages closest to the Mouth of Swords and succeeds on a difficulty 3 Intellect-based task discovers the following:

• Over the past year, a figure wearing a dusty grey cloak, possibly human, has sometimes been seen traveling across the plain that lies before the Mouth of Swords. No one has ever seen the cloaked figure up close. (The figure was the Dustman, checking on the kidnapped eggs.)

Tidy State of Repair: *Given the active nature of Myth Keeper (area 3) and the various creatures under its thrall, the chambers beyond the entrance are clear of dust, vandalism, and detritus, unless noted to the contrary.*

MOVING THE ADVENTURE FORWARD

Ardeyn is a world in its own right, and PCs could easily become sidetracked from the main arc of *The Dark Spiral*. And that's okay! If the characters want to explore Citadel Hazurrium, shop in its markets, join an adventuring company, explore the Path of the Dead, and so on, you should accommodate them—at least, up to a point. As the GM, it's your job to make sure that events don't bog down or that one player doesn't dictate the actions of the rest of the group.

You can help things along by using one of the following tactics. Even if the adventure doesn't go off track, consider introducing one or more of the following events to remind the characters of the larger scope of The Strange.

• A courier from the Estate arrives, asking the PCs to report back on the status of their mission to roll up the spiral dust trade.

• A message reaches the PCs that the Estate base is under attack (as described in Intermission 1).

• A quickened elite kro goon assassin in the employ of Don Wyclef tracks the PCs to Ardeyn.

Intermission 1, page 23

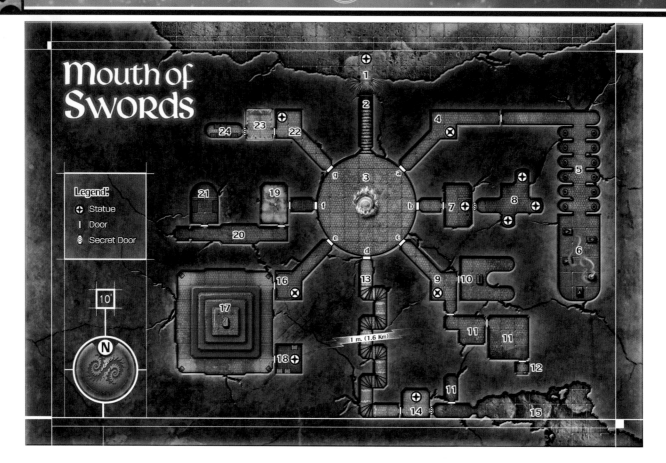

Mouth of Swords

Legend:
- ⊕ Statue
- | Door
- $ Secret Door

10'

N

1 m. (1.6 Km)

1. OUTSIDE THE MOUTH OF SWORDS

When the characters arrive at the Mouth of Swords, it's not easy to miss.

read aloud

A half mile or more from the line of ridges stretching to the east, a lone outcrop erupts from the plain. Its steep cliff face is punctured by a gaping cavity. Hundreds of rusted, disintegrating swords are bolted around the opening, their tips bare and pointing menacingly inward, so that the cavity almost resembles the mouth of a beast with hundreds of decaying iron teeth. Standing before the opening is an eroded stone sculpture of a humanoid in robes, but the head is missing.

If the PCs examine the area around the mouth, they find evidence of several older camps (campfires, discarded equipment, bones, and so on) going back decades. The place has been visited by groups of adventurers for years. A dedicated search reveals that the most recent camp was probably abandoned only a few months back.

Those same searches also quickly recover the cracked but intact head of the statue—a qephilim head—lying in tall grass near the entrance.

Statue: The statue is weathered and partly defaced, but it retains a vestige of ancient magic. If the head is found in the nearby underbrush and put back in place, the statue's mouth animates and offers the following warning to anyone standing before it:

"Enter here, and die. The swords adorning the Mouth were taken from the remains of those who failed to heed my prophecy."

The statue repeats the same warning to each new individual who stands facing it within immediate range, but never to the same person twice.

Entrance: The opening is so beset with rusting swords that passing through requires a difficulty 2 Speed-based roll to work through (or jump beyond) the points without getting a severe cut inflicting 3 points of damage. A close examination of the affixed swords reveals that they are spiked in the cliffside by long iron nails.

2. STAIRS

read aloud

Stairs carved with all manner of faintly glowing runes ascend higher into the cliff. A gently flickering light, like fire, reflects down from farther above.

Characters with the foci Shepherds the Dead or Practices Soul Sorcery or who have a similar connection to the magic of Ardeyn recognize the runes as a sort of spirit barrier. "Unclothed" spirits have a difficult time passing down (or up) the stairs. In effect, the stairs seem like they serve to keep spirits bottled up. However, PCs with spirits of their own to shepherd must succeed on a difficulty 2 Intellect-based task to get their companion creatures across the barrier.

3. MYTH KEEPER
A wrath lord calling itself Myth Keeper controls access to the seven locked doors in this chamber via the magical fire pit in the center and the ring on its finger that controls the flame.

read aloud
This large, plazalike chamber has a high domed roof. The floor is a mosaic of spiraling tile originating from a large copper bowl fixed to the floor at the center. A tongue of red flame burns along the edge of the copper vessel, rather than in the center, without apparent fuel source. Seven massive stone doors stand closed around the edges of the chamber, each one covered with relief carvings. Near the fire pit, a hooded figure in dirty, tattered yellow robes stands unmoving.

The yellow-robed figure is a wrath lord calling itself Myth Keeper. Beneath its disintegrating garments, it's only partly substantial.

Myth Keeper: Upon noticing the PCs, Myth Keeper asks in sepulchral tones, "What treasure have you brought for me to keep safe?"

If the PCs don't understand, Myth Keeper explains its role. "I keep safe treasures from the Age of Myth for a fee."

Really, Myth Keeper stores anything brought to it if payment is sufficient (100 crowns, on average). The wrath lord gives a receipt for each deposit (a tiny, unique clay figurine of a qephilim) and will retrieve a stored item if the receipt is presented to it again. Myth Keeper calls the complex the "Vault of Keeping."

Myth Keeper will divulge some of what is stored here in a boastful sort of way, but it never reveals behind which door any particular treasure lies, or how any individual item is specifically stored or guarded. If asked about Donna Ilsa's eggs, Myth Keeper confirms they are indeed safely stored. He also describes

The dome height is 40 feet (12 m).

Show 'Em: *Myth Keeper, Image G, page 94*

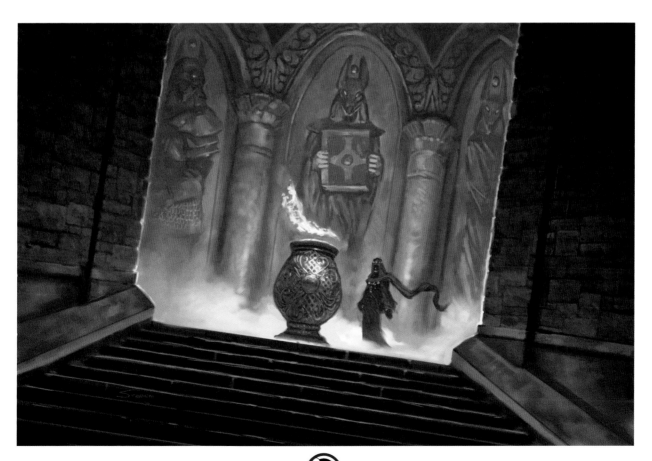

the "Stranger" who deposited the eggs: "A creature in the shape of a man, but who never was one, hidden beneath a cloak somewhat like my own, but grey and stained with blue dust." (Myth Keeper is referring to the Dustman but doesn't know his name.)

If it becomes clear to Myth Keeper that the PCs do not have a treasure to store, it tells them to be off. If it becomes clear that the PCs are there to *steal* something stored in its keeping, it attacks.

Secret Life: As a wrath lord, Myth Keeper keeps its mental focus in a qephilim clay figure hidden in room 7 under a loose piece of tile. Unless that figurine is found and destroyed, Myth Keeper can't be permanently killed—it always reforms again at the next midnight.

Ring of Fire: Myth Keeper wears a seven-sided ring on one partly insubstantial finger. When it (or anyone) turns the ring, the flame in the copper bowl moves a certain distance corresponding to the number of turns. Whichever door the flame ends up nearest to becomes unlocked; all the other doors are locked. Only one door is unlocked at a time. When a door changes state from locked to unlocked, the sound of a metal bolt disengaging shakes the entire chamber.

Killing Myth Keeper: If the PCs kill Myth Keeper twice, the third time it regenerates (assuming the characters haven't found and destroyed its secret life), it might collect Rimush from room 21 so that it has backup the next time it faces the intruders.

Copper Bowl and Circling Flame: This magical feature is fixed in place and is linked with the ring of fire worn by Myth Keeper. The flame circles the edge of the bowl as determined by the wearer of the ring, and the doors around the chamber are either locked or unlocked depending on which door the flame is closest to. Snuffing out the flame is possible, but it returns unless the PCs manage to excavate the 1-ton (907 kg) copper bowl from its stone foundation.

Seven Doors: Each of the seven doors in the chamber corresponds with one of the seven vanished Incarnations of the Maker. Unless a door is unlocked, it's a difficulty 8 task to pick, break, or otherwise bypass the door. If a door is unlocked using the ring of fire, opening the door is as easy as pushing. The relief carving on each door is as follows.

A. *Death:* A qephilim dressed in the robes of an umber judge surrounded by a mist of spirits.

B. *Desire:* A qephilim dressed and posed in a position some might call alluring.

C. *Lore:* A qephilim in simple robes and spectacles clutching a massive tome.

D. *Silence:* A monitor in simple robes with one finger to its lips.

E. *War:* A qephilim in full plate armor with a massive talwar (a greatsword with a broad, curved blade).

F. *Commerce:* A qephilim in rich robes holding an elaborately decorated chest that is bursting with crowns.

G. *Law:* A qephilim in magisterial robes reading from an unfurled scroll so long that its ends wind about the creature's legs.

WRATH LORD   5 (15)

Spirits who lose their way to the Night Vault become bodiless spirits of rage and loss called wraths (or spirits of wrath). A rare few hold onto the sense of who and what they were before dying by "adopting" a few bits of physical substance to act as an anchor to the world. These spirits are wrath lords. A wrath lord usually requires two such objects: one piece of clothing or another garment that helps give the creature shape, and an amulet, hood, hat, crown, or other charm that provides clarity of mind.

Wrath lords also choose an undertaking. Unlike their lesser kin, wrath lords are not mindless engines of destruction. Each one adheres to a specific goal, task, or duty that, like its adopted physical anchors, holds it from slipping away. Often that undertaking is guarding a tomb, shrine, library, treasury, or similar location, but sometimes wrath lords choose less isolating tasks.

Motive: Research, guardianship, or another ongoing task

Environment (Ardeyn | Magic): Almost anywhere

Health: 15

Damage Inflicted: 5 points

Armor: 1

Movement: Short when flying

Combat: A wrath lord can attack with its touch, which rots flesh and drains life. Its preferred tactic is to throw back its hood and fix its death gaze on foes within short range and within immediate range of each other. Targets who see this flaring spirit light from the wrath lord's gaping mouth and eyes must succeed on an Intellect defense roll or suffer 5 points of life-draining damage that ignores Armor. The wrath lord can

---

Donna Ilsa's five eggs are distributed across five rooms: 6, 8, 18, 19, and 23.

GM Intrusion: *The wrath lord unleashes six spirits of wrath from its cloak.*

A wrath lord chooses a new name to go with its chosen task and forgets the name it had as a living being.

> *Court of Sleep qephilim once rode deathless chargers to track wandering spirits. They could also handle a charger's disembodied horn safely and use it to mark those whom the Incarnation of Death had selected to die.*

make this attack once every other round. (If a PC averts his eyes from the wrath lord, the difficulty of Intellect rolls to avoid the death gaze is reduced by two steps, but the difficulty of all attack and other defense tasks associated with the wrath lord is increased by two steps.)

- A wrath lord can become fully insubstantial, including its physical garment and any other possessions. After it does so, it can't change state again until its next turn. While insubstantial, it can't affect or be affected by anything (except for spiritslaying weapons and attacks), and it can't use its death gaze. It can pass through solid matter without hindrance, though many magical wards can keep it at bay.
- While a wrath lord remains partly insubstantial (its normal state), it can affect and be affected by others normally.
- If a wrath lord is destroyed, it spontaneously regenerates within six to twelve hours unless all the physical objects it uses to give itself shape and clarity of mind are found and destroyed (usually a garment it wears, plus an object it has hidden elsewhere, which is often called its secret life).

Interaction: Wrath lords speak in sepulchral voices, and they might negotiate, but one will never agree to forsake any part of its chosen undertaking.

Use: The PCs are approached by a wrath lord whose special undertaking is "exploration" and asked to find a relic in the Chaosphere.

Loot: Most wrath lords have a cypher or two, and possibly an artifact.

4. HORNED HORSE

read aloud

Floor tiles spiral out from a statue embedded in the corner of this area: a horselike creature rears, its head high and its hooves flashing, though time and perhaps vandalism have robbed it of its left front leg. A spiraling horn erupts from the center of its forehead like a

spike. Unlike the rest of the sculpture, the horn appears to be carved of bone.

The "unicorn" sculpture fixed in place in the chamber isn't magical, but the horn has unusual qualities. The horn is actually the quiescent, larval form of a deathless charger. A simple twist will remove the horn from the statue. Doing so summons the deathless charger the horn belongs to, as well as the saddlebags stuffed with the treasure that Myth Keeper stored within.

Saddlebags: If the deathless charger is defeated, it leaves behind its horn and two large saddlebags. One bag has three cyphers: a level 3 manipulation beam; a level 5 Intellect booster, and a level 4 ray emitter (command). The other saddlebag contains a fist-sized peridot and at least 300 crowns.

DEATHLESS CHARGER   5 (15)

A deathless charger is summoned when its disembodied horn is found and handled. Though the charger is deathless itself, it brings death to other creatures. Charger victims rarely realize what has killed them. Survivors describe a terrifying, horselike beast with a bone horn as the implement of their friend's death, a horn that moments earlier was not attached to a ton of bestial fury.

When not wed with its horn, a deathless charger is a bodiless spirit racing along the Night Vault's Roads of Sorrow, visible to the living as hardly more than the suggestion of a shape and a cool wind. Seeing one pass by is considered an omen of doom.

Motive: Kill those marked for death
Environment (Ardeyn | Magic): A deathless charger's disembodied horn can be found almost anywhere.
Health: 18
Damage Inflicted: Varies; see Combat
Armor: 1
Movement: Short
Modifications: First surprise attack as level 7; Speed defense as level 4.

Manipulation beam, page 321

Intellect booster, page 320

Ray emitter, page 325

Spirit of wrath, page 292

GM Intrusion: *The deathless charger fades into mist, leaving its disembodied horn behind.*

Combat: A deathless charger usually begins a combat with surprise, appearing suddenly attached to its previously disembodied horn, and as if having charged full tilt to that point. This melee attack is made as if the charger were a level 7 creature; on a success, the charger deals 7 points of damage.

On subsequent rounds, the deathless charger can attack with two hooves as its action against one or two creatures in immediate range, or charge a creature that is beyond immediate range but within short range. When it charges another creature using its horn as a weapon, a successful attack deals 2 additional points of damage (for a total of 5 points) that ignores Armor. The charger can charge as its attack only every other round.

If a deathless charger would be killed, it dissipates instead, leaving only its horn behind (as well as any rider or accoutrements).

Interaction: Deathless chargers were made as servants of Death, and little can sway them from attempting to kill whosoever has been marked by their disembodied horns.

Spirit of wrath, page 292

5. Aisle of Urns

read aloud

This long hallway is composed of a series of facing alcoves. Each alcove contains a heavily carved stone urn stoppered with lead. An inscription on each reads, "GUARDIAN."

If the PCs leave well enough alone in this chamber (and in area 6), nothing happens. But if they open one or more of the urns, necromancy flares and the ashes stored within each urn begin calling spirits of wrath. The summoning call occurs over the course of two rounds and is accompanied by sepulchral moaning, flashes of green light alternating with utter darkness, and the ominous sound of lead stoppers popping off the remaining urns.

After two rounds, six spirits of wrath appear from the mouths of six random urns. Every round after that, another 1d6 spirits appear. This continues for as long as the PCs are present in areas 4, 5, or 6, or as long as the urns remain unstoppered. Stoppering an urn requires an action. For each two urns stoppered (or smashed), one fewer wrath is generated in the following round.

Inside the Urns: PCs who break open the urns by smashing them discover that the dust hides one of the following treasures.

1	Level 3 reflex enhancer
2	Emerald (50 crowns)
3	Gold ring (25 crowns)
4	Level 6 null field
5	Level 5 radiation spike
6	Amber ring (20 crowns)
7	Level 5 stim
8	Level 7 telepathic bond
9	Coil of endless rope
10	Book of Ardeyn lore (asset to knowledge rolls)
11	Ruby (200 crowns)
12	Clay qephilim figure (receipt for room 23)

6. SARCOPHAGI TREASURE ROOM

read aloud

A layer of water covers the ceiling, defying gravity, but reflecting a grand room beneath inlaid with crystal tiles and ivory fixtures. Four large sarcophagi are scattered about the chamber, each one forged of dark iron and featuring a demonic face and form relief carved in its surface.

A hulking black iron urn issues a thin stream of smoke, and on it is inscribed the words "BREATH OF LOTAN."

ARTIFACT: COIL OF ENDLESS ROPE

Level: 1d6
Form: Coil of rope
Effect: The coil of rope can be let out at a rate of 50 feet (15 m) per round; however, no end to the rope can be found no matter how long the user uncoils it. The rope retains its incredible length until recoiled or until it becomes depleted. Each hour the rope's length remains extended past 50 feet requires a depletion roll.
Depletion: 1 in d20

PCs who examine the area and succeed on a difficulty 2 Intellect-based task note that in addition to the fact that the ceiling is drowned, the entrance contains a pocket door of iron that is currently retracted, with no obvious mechanism for controlling it.

Drowned Ceiling: If the PCs specifically examine the room through its reflection, everything looks the same except for the urn, which instead looks like a crouching, quivering, demonic humanoid bound in black

Show 'Em: Reflected Room of Kings, Image H, page 94

Reflex enhancer, page 326

Null field, page 324

Radiation spike, page 325

Stim, page 328

Telepathic bond, page 329

If the clay qephilim figure is presented to Myth Keeper, it retrieves the treasure from one of the chests (PCs' choice) stored in room 23 without complaint.

iron chains, with smoke issuing from its nostrils. The ceiling is also part of the water trap.

Water Trap: If any of the sarcophagi in the room are opened, a magical trap is triggered: an iron panel slides across the entrance, sealing the chamber. (If the PCs found the pocket door and spiked it open or otherwise disabled it, they succeed in delaying the door from sliding shut for 1d6 rounds before the magic overcomes any physical intervention.) Once sealed, opening the door requires three successful difficulty 5 tasks; the PCs are free to try whatever seems reasonable to gain those successes, including physical brawn, lockpicking, or something else.

Simultaneously, water begins streaming down from the ceiling in great rivulets, filling the entire chamber within ten minutes (without leaving an air space above).

If the door is unsealed, the water runs back to its initial position on the ceiling. Otherwise, the trap doesn't reset for one hour, and PCs stuck inside hopefully remember that three of them working together can try to translate to safety before they drown.

Sarcophagi: The four sarcophagi contain the following stored treasures:

First: 300 crowns' worth of silver, amber, and gold coins.

Second: Amber statue of a beautiful woman worth 300 crowns.

Third: Five anoetic cyphers (two level 5 analeptics, a level 6 condition remover, and two level 4 effort enhancers) and a leather pouch containing two tiny clay pots stoppered with wax. Each pot holds one dose of spiral dust.

Fourth: One of Donna Ilsa's kidnapped eggs in a leather sack.

Smoking Urn: A thin stream of vapor issues from a vent in this large urn's lead stopper, which has been sealed with wax (the wax must be burned or pried off to remove the seal). If the stopper is removed, a demon of Lotan emerges, holding a weapon engraved with glowing runes denoting spiritslaying (the weapon is a medium scimitar of spiritslaying). The demon, whose name is Gultrea, is bound to protect the weapon, but it offers the PCs another way to get it without having to fight: if one of the PCs volunteers to be the demon's vessel, the characters can have the weapon freely. The demon is good to its word, at least at first. Being a demon, it eventually tries to exploit the situation.

Grenade (cell-disrupting), page 318

Analeptic, page 313

Condition remover, 314

Effort enhancer, page 316

Spiral dust, page 156

Demon of Lotan, page 265

Spiritslaying weapon, page 189

7. SHRINE OF DESIRE

read aloud

Blue tiles on the floor spiral out from the fixed statue of a female qephilim. The sculpture has a grace, beauty, and breathtaking artistry that captures the eye and heart. A few figures sit along the side walls, but their presence is incidental to the smooth lines and motion of the statue.

The sculpture of the Incarnation of Desire is a magical trap. Anyone in the chamber longer than a few rounds who gazes upon the statue and fails a difficulty 4 Intellect defense roll becomes magically fascinated and will move only to find a better vantage point for looking at the statue. The effect lasts until someone who is not under the geas of the statue spends a few actions slapping a victim out of his daze, or until the statue is physically covered with a cloth, tarp, or similar barrier.

Slumped Figures: Three dead humans, dried and mummified from their long stay in the chamber gazing at Desire, sit slumped against the side walls. Most of their belongings have rotted long past usability, but PC looters recover a total of 100 crowns, a level 5 cell-disrupting grenade cypher, and a partial map of the Mouth of Swords complex that shows rooms 1, 2, 3, 4, 7, 9, and 16.

Loose Tile: A loose piece of tile (difficulty 5 Intellect-based roll to find) covers a cavity containing a small burlap pouch. In the pouch is a qephilim clay figure that looks like a receipt that redeems stored treasure from Myth Keeper. However, the figure is the source of the wrath lord's life, and if it's destroyed, Myth Keeper will not regenerate the next time it is killed.

Secret Door: If the PCs search the room and succeed on a difficulty 4 Intellect-based roll, they find a secret door behind the statue of Desire that connects to room 8.

8. THREE ASPECTS

read aloud

Three large alcoves in this chamber each hold a unique sculpture. All of them are beautiful, but each one seems to focus on the beauty of a particular characteristic. One statue is of a particularly fit and muscular nude human male throwing a weighty hammer. Another statue is of a qephilim (sex uncertain) apparently evading two swinging pendulums with preternatural grace. The last statue is of a female human consulting a tome while writing sorcerous runes or mathematical script on a long piece of parchment.

If approached, each statue animates and offers its hand to the supplicant. If the supplicant places her hand in the statue's hand, she takes damage from one of her Pools, but afterward, the statue produces the object it keeps safe as if from thin air.

Hammer Thrower: 10 points of Might damage; statue produces a sapphire worth 200 crowns.

Pendulum Evader: 10 points of Speed damage; statue produces one of Donna Ilsa's kidnapped eggs.

Problem Solver: 10 points of Intellect damage; statue produces an iron chest. The chest is locked with a level 5 mechanism and protected by a level 5 trap (if not deactivated, the trap deals 5 points of fire damage to the person who opens it and everyone within immediate range). Inside the chest is the Spellbook of the Amber Mage.

9. RIDDLING SHRINE OF LORE

read aloud

The tiles on the floor of this chamber appear to be letters of the alphabet in random assortment. The statue inside looks like a more fully rendered version of the relief carving on the door leading into this chamber: an angelic qephilim clutching a tome of lore.

If approached, the statue animates just enough to pose a riddle to the PCs. The statue knows countless riddles plucked from endless recursions. One of the riddles it might pose is provided below. If a PC answers the riddle incorrectly, nothing untoward occurs. If a PC answers the riddle correctly, the door to room 10 is unlocked.

Riddle: A lost spirit sought to escape the Court of Sleep but wasn't privy to the test of lore required that day. The spirit observed a few other souls that managed to escape the umber judges. When the first soul petitioned to be freed from its captivity, the judge intoned "twelve," and the soul answered "six." When the second soul petitioned, the judge whispered "six," and the soul answered

"three." The lost spirit saw a pattern, so it approached the guardian judge and petitioned for freedom. The umber judge proclaimed "ten," and the lost spirit answered "five." But this answer was incorrect, and instead of being freed, the spirit was consigned to the umber wolves. Why was the spirit incorrect? **Answer:** The correct answer was "three" because there are three letters in the word "ten."

10. ESSENCE TRANSFER

The iron door connecting this room to room 9 is normally locked with a level 7 mechanism. If picked or opened by answering a riddle in room 9, the door remains unlocked for up to an hour before swinging closed and locking once more.

read aloud

A silvered altar stands in the room between two deep alcoves. A jade-handled lever attached to the altar is thrown all the way to the left.

The altar is the treasure that the statue in room 9 protected. The altar is portable, but only barely (it weighs as much as a full-grown human in plate armor).

If a creature stands in one alcove, an object (a figurine, a statue, a sword, a doll, a big rock—anything, really) is placed in the other alcove, and the lever is thrown, the creature must make a difficulty 3 Intellect defense roll. Failure means its mind is transferred into the object. If the creature and object are returned to the alcoves, throwing the lever the other way reverses the process.

If this happens to a PC, the character whose mind is transferred into an object loses the ability to move but can speak telepathically to anything touching or holding the object that has become his body. The PC is allowed another Intellect defense roll 24 hours after the transfer, but if he fails the second roll, he should hope that his companions choose to reverse the process, or he is stuck—at least until he translates to another recursion. However, if he translates back to Ardeyn later, he'll probably become the object again.

The body of a living creature whose mind is transferred into an object falls into something like a coma. The body can survive in this fashion for about a week without care.

Spellbook of the Amber Mage, page 189

11. Empty

read aloud

Dust collects in the corners of this empty chamber.

Spirit of wrath, page 292

Myth Keeper isn't at full capacity, and some of its treasure vaults are vacant. On the other hand, each empty chamber has a chance to have collected wandering spirits of wrath. When the PCs first find an empty chamber marked 11 on the map, roll a d20.

On a roll of 1, the chamber contains 2d6 spirits of wrath, which initially appear to be faintly glowing relief carvings on the wall. If disturbed, the "carvings" flow off the wall to become partly substantial but quite real threats.

Rimush, page 63

On a roll of 2–4, the PCs encounter Rimush the golem (normally in room 21), clearing out spirits of wrath that have taken up residence in the chamber.

12. Closet

read aloud

Dust collects in the corners of this small room. A metal box sits on an otherwise empty shelf.

Inside the metal box is a thick packet of folded parchment with seven simple line drawings of humans, qephilim, demons, hydra, and other creatures of Ardeyn. The only hint of an explanation is an eighth piece of parchment folded in with the others, which contains no art but has the words "Seven soul gems?" written on it.

Night Vault, page 183

Roads of Sorrow, page 183

Umber wolf, page 295

13. Descent

read aloud

At the bend in the corridor ahead are stairs leading down. They are carved with all manner of faintly glowing runes.

The first set of stairs past the door is like the stairs in room 2 and serves as a barrier to spirits.

If the PCs continue down the snaking path, which alternates between a corridor and stairs, it plunges deeper with no apparent side exits. The stairs grow more dusty, too, as if they haven't been used or cleaned in years (Myth Keeper cleans the used chambers in the depository). After more than a mile (2 km)

of descent, the stairs finally level off, and the corridor ends at the door to room 14.

14. Another Horned Horse

read aloud

The sculpture of a rearing horse with a single horn on its forehead stands alone here. Words inscribed on the wall opposite the statue read, "JOURNEY NOT INTO THE NIGHT VAULT LEST UMBER WOLVES TEAR YOUR SOUL FROM YOUR LIVING BODY AND DEVOUR YOUR STILL-THRASHING SPIRIT."

The horn of the rearing horse is not bone (as in room 4) but metal; this statue doesn't host a deathless charger. However, it does have a level 5 mechanism.

If the horn is rotated to the left, the secret door on the east wall slides open. If the horn is rotated to the right, a piercing scream blares from the statue's mouth, and all creatures within short range that fail a Might defense roll suffer 5 points of damage from the flesh-ripping audible intensity of the blast.

Finding the secret door without turning the horn requires a difficulty 5 Intellect-based task.

15. Roads of Sorrow

read aloud

The worked stone passage gives way to a rough, natural subterranean tunnel that snakes down to the east.

The Night Vault of Ardeyn is made up of tunnels and vaults, collectively called the Roads of Sorrow. This passage is one of the many surface connections to the deeper tunnels. To travel it is to journey beneath Ardeyn and beyond the scope of this adventure. PCs who look down the natural tunnel might hear the distant, hair-raising howl of hunting umber wolves as a cold breeze out of nowhere ruffles their clothing.

16. Masterful Shrine of War

read aloud

Black tiles with white highlights on the floor spiral out from the fixed statue of a male qephilim in full plate armor bearing a massive blade. The sculpture captures fierceness, power, and breathtaking mastery. Racks of weapons of various kinds are affixed to two walls.

Someone sensitive to magic who examines the chamber and succeeds on a difficulty 2 Intellect-based task determines that some kind of spell infiltrates the room, and it's strongest near the weapon racks.

This chamber's door to room 17 is normally unlocked (and room 17 empty). However, if someone takes a weapon from a rack, the door to room 17 slams shut if it was open and locks with a click. (A difficulty 7 Might- or Intellect-based task is required to bash it open or pick the lock, respectively.) The statue in the chamber intones, "Your challenge is accepted. Victory is your only option." Two sark are summoned to room 17, as described in that room's entry. Simultaneously, if the creature that took the weapon from the rack fails a difficulty 5 Intellect defense roll, she is teleported to the base of the pyramid in room 17. If she succeeds on the roll, she is not teleported, but the sark are summoned to the pyramid either way.

Multiple weapons taken from the racks could result in multiple targets being teleported to room 17 and more sark being summoned. The door to room 17 doesn't unlock (of its own accord) until all the sark summoned there are defeated.

If the characters successfully bash open or pick the lock to the door to room 17, choosing another weapon from the racks relocks it as described above.

Weapon Racks: The weapon racks contain multiple instances of all the weapons listed under Ardeyn Equipment in the corebook.

Door to Room 17: This door is made of iron and hides a level 7 mechanism (see room 17).

17. MOUTH OF SWORDS ARENA

read aloud
This wide chamber is brilliantly lit by massive lamps on iron posts set at the four corners. An imposing stone step pyramid occupies most of the chamber, leaving only a 10-foot (3 m) lane around the pyramid base. Each ledge of the pyramid is 5 feet (2 m) wide, and each step rises 5 feet (2 m) to the next, climbing a total of four steps. The pyramid, floor, and ceiling are covered with inscribed runes and wide circles that glimmer with eldritch light. At the very top of the pyramid, a bronze altar squats.

PCs who enter this chamber without teleporting in from room 16 find the step pyramid empty of creatures. Those who trigger the spell and enter by teleportation are greeted

Show 'Em: *Mouth of Swords Arena, Image I, page 95*

Ardeyn Equipment, page 89

by summoned sark.

Step Pyramid: Climbing each 5-foot (2 m) tall step is a difficulty 2 Might task. A search of the pyramid uncovers a few bones from past fights (human, qephilim, and sark), though Myth Keeper generally keeps the pyramid tidy.

Summoned Sark: If sark are summoned while any PCs are in room 17, they appear in a random location on the pyramid, but always higher than the PCs (if possible). The sark target PCs who are not on their level with ranged weapons (bows, each with seven red-fletched arrows) and engage in melee combat with PCs who climb to the same ledge. A sark standing above a climbing PC gets a free shot at stamping on the character's fingers, or a kick in the face as the character comes over the top. The primary goal of the sark is to keep the PCs (or any intruding creature) from reaching the altar on top of the step pyramid. Their secondary goal is to kill the intruders.

Door to Room 16. This iron door is connected to a hidden level 7 mechanism. The door shuts and locks when sark are summoned to the arena. It unlocks once those sark are dead.

Altar: The bronze altar on top of the pyramid has a bronze dial with three settings. It's normally set to the central setting. The dial is connected to a hidden level 5 mechanism.

Central Setting: A cuneiform-like symbol of a step pyramid designates this setting, which is the neutral setting. The dial returns to this setting a few minutes after it is changed (unless damaged or held in place).

Left Setting: The cuneiform-like symbol designating this setting is a simple rectangle on its side. If the dial is clicked to this setting, the entire top level of the step pyramid goes into freefall and drops 40 feet (12 m) into a pit beneath the center of the pyramid, hitting the bottom of the pit with a crashing boom. PCs standing on the level when it falls must succeed on a difficulty 5 Speed defense roll or fall the same number of feet (and take 4 points of damage that ignores Armor). A round later, the mechanism clicks, and the top level snaps back into place. This has the unfortunate side effect of flinging PCs who fail a second difficulty 5 Speed defense roll into the ceiling, followed by an inevitable plunge back onto the top level (inflicting 4 more points of damage that ignores Armor). At this point, the dial clicks back to the central setting.

Right Setting: The cuneiform-like symbol

designating this setting is a simple vertical rectangle. If the dial is turned to this setting, the door to room 18 clicks loudly as it is unlocked (unless the PCs managed to unlock it previously). After an hour, the dial returns to the central setting if not held or disabled, and the door closes (if it is open) and locks.

18. BOUNTIFUL SHRINE OF WAR
The iron door to this chamber is locked (level 7 mechanism) unless the dial on top of the pyramid in room 17 is turned to the right setting, which unlocks the door.

read aloud
Black tiles with white highlights on the floor spiral out from the fixed statue of a male qephilim in full plate armor bearing a massive blade. The sculpture captures fierceness, power, and breathtaking mastery. Three chests inlaid with pearl and ebony are stored in the chamber near the statue. A couple of mummified remains of humans lie like discarded logs along one wall.

Except for the danger of staying too long, the PCs are free to rifle through the unlocked chests without triggering further repercussions.

Chest 1: This chest contains three bottles of four-hundred-year-old wine from the lost vineyards of Sanurfa. Each bottle is worth a few hundred crowns to a connoisseur. Otherwise, it's just very good wine.

Chest 2: This chest contains the head of a heavy maul. On the head is inscribed (in the Maker's Tongue) "Grandfather's maul." Possibly invaluable to whoever asked it to be stored here, the maul has no other apparent significance.

Chest 3: This chest contains one of Donna Ilsa's eggs, packed in sawdust. It also contains two anoetic cyphers: a level 6 ray emitter (fear) and a level 5 strength boost.

Bodies: The bodies are those of adventurers who made it into this chamber, only to linger too long and become trapped when the door to room 17 closed and locked itself. They died of starvation and have been stripped of valuables.

19. GLASS URN

read aloud
An iron tripod is bolted to the floor in the center of this chamber. The tripod's claws

Ray emitter (fear),
page 325

Strength boost,
page 329

Multiphasic module,
page 323

hold a glass vessel about 4 feet tall and 2 feet in diameter (1.2 by 0.6 m) filled with misty condensation. Steam rolls off the vessel, covering the floor.

PCs in the chamber immediately note that it's colder here than in the rest of the complex, and those sensitive to magic who succeed on a difficulty 3 Intellect-based task detect spells of containment around the glass vessel.

Touching the supernaturally cold vessel inflicts 1 point of damage, accompanied by a violent, telepathic scream of anger. If a PC attempts to strike up a conversation with the telepathic entity in the vessel, she must call on all her powers of persuasion (a difficulty 4 Intellect-based task) and hold her hand on the vessel (which inflicts 1 point of cold damage only for another round or so, if the PC calms the entity).

Entity in the Urn: The entity in the urn is a ngeshtin, a creature of winter, but one that enjoys warming itself with wine. If a PC achieves good relations with the ngeshtin, it indicates that it guards two treasures on Myth Keeper's behalf: a large egg (one of Donna Ilsa's eggs) and a small chest that contains a level 4 multiphasic module cypher. The ngeshtin goes so far as to suggest that it will give up one or both treasures in return for a jug of wine. If the PCs so bribe the creature, the offered wine disappears, and one or both treasures materialize on the floor of the chamber, each coated in a rime of ice crystal.

The only other way to get the stored treasures out of the glass urn is to smash it. This causes the treasures to materialize on the floor but also releases the ngeshtin, which attacks the PCs who destroyed its home.

NGESHTIN   6 (18)

Ngeshtins inhabit glaciers, frozen lakes, and winter storms. Though completely physical while manifest, ngeshtins possess something of a spiritual nature, and they can appear seemingly out of nowhere when the seasons change or in the presence of something exceptionally cold.

A ngeshtin looks somewhat like a qephilim from the waist up (if a qephilim's fingers were tipped with claws of sharp ice) and like a massive snake from the waist down. Its entire body smells of pine needles and is covered in white scales, frost, and steaming cold. Quick and dexterous despite its chilled body, a ngeshtin "stands" about 9 feet (3 m) tall on its

coiled tail, but one measured from head to tail tip would be much longer.

Ngeshtins have a special fondness for the fermented gifts of the vine. In some parts of Ardeyn, ngeshtins are known more as spirits of wine than of winter. The cold that ngeshtins emit doesn't adversely affect wine of any kind.

Motive: Defense

Environment (Ardeyn | Magic): Anywhere, but usually in cold areas

Health: 18

Damage Inflicted: 6 points

Armor: 2

Movement: Short

Modifications: Speed defense as level 4 due to size.

GM Intrusion: *The ngeshtin breathes a blast of cold air, and instead of dealing damage, it creates a dome of translucent ice around one PC within short range. The dome has 2 points of Armor and can take 12 points of damage before shattering. Lifting the dome high enough to get out is a difficulty 3 Might-based task.*

Combat: A ngeshtin can use its claws in melee or spend an action to first fashion a massive curved sword (a talwar) of ice, condensed from moisture in the air. Attacks with the talwar deal 2 additional points of damage (for a total of 8 points of damage).

Once every other round, a ngeshtin can breathe a blast of cold air within short range at a group of targets in immediate range of each other. Targets who make a successful Speed defense roll still take 1 point of damage.

A ngeshtin can fashion basic objects out of ice condensed and frozen from moisture in the air. Such objects can be no larger than a human and could include a shield, a chair, a solid sculpture, and so on. The ngeshtin can also use this ability to seal an opening or bridge a gap.

A ngeshtin is vulnerable to unexpected heat. Fire damage dealt to a ngeshtin causes it to lose its next action, but only the first time during any given combat.

A ngeshtin regenerates 3 points of health per round if any part of its body is touching a large mass of ice (or is dipped in a large body of snow or ice water).

Interaction: Ngeshtins communicate telepathically with creatures they can see within 100 feet (30 m). Different ngeshtins have different goals, but most are willing to subordinate those goals in return for good wine.

Use: The PCs are asked to bring a gift of wine to a meeting with someone of importance in Ardeyn. When the characters go to procure the wine, they find that a ngeshtin has made a prior claim.

Loot: If wine is of value to the PCs, a ngeshtin usually has a couple of bottles in its hoard.

20. TRAPPED HALLWAY

read aloud

Red letters race across the cobbled floor of the hallway, back and forth along its length. At the west end of the passage, an arch opens into darkness.

The racing letters are composed of ephemeral spell-light. The alphabet is recognizably in the Maker's Tongue, but the movement makes it hard to decipher the message. A successful difficulty 5 Intellect-based roll reveals the message: "The darkness hungers."

A spell obviously suffuses the hallway.

Anyone other than Myth Keeper or Rimush the golem who moves more than 30 feet (9 m) down the passage triggers the effect: the apparent plane of gravity shifts 90 degrees in an instant. The shift lasts until no living creature remains in rooms 20 or 21.

Pit of Area 20: When the trap triggers, what was west is now down. PCs in the hallway who fail a difficulty 5 Speed defense roll (or who were not holding onto something fixed in place) fall into the arch at the end of the hall. The distance they fall is equal to wherever they were standing, which you can round to 60 feet (18 m) for each character, so each PC takes 6 points of damage.

The arch at the end of the hall opens into a shallow cavity in the west wall, but when the trap triggers, the cavity becomes a well of absolute darkness in the floor. Each round that a living creature remains within 10 feet (3 m) of the cavity, a lesser inkling curls out like vapor and attacks the closest living target.

Climbing out of the "pit" of what was a hallway is a difficulty 4 Might-based task. Gravity is normal in rooms 21 and 19, so reaching those rooms means the ordeal is over.

21. WORK ROOM

read aloud

This chamber is something of a jumble. Stone sculptures in various stages of completion are scattered about the room. A large workbench heaped with rusted swords stands against one wall near a rack filled with all manner of stone working tools, cleaning implements, and other oddments. Five large iron pails sit beneath the workbench. A second workbench is littered with tiny clay figures. A brilliant point of red light hangs in midair over the workbench, illuminating the entire room in crimson.

Unless the PCs have previously encountered it, one of the "half-finished" sculptures in the chamber is actually a golem named Rimush. The golem doesn't move unless the PCs identify it (an Intellect-based task for someone specifically examining the sculptures) or mess about with other objects in the room. Rimush serves the needs of Myth Keeper, which is usually repair and maintenance of the Mouth of Swords. If commanded by Myth Keeper, it will also attack the PCs, even if the characters previously established cordial relations.

 Lesser inkling, page 273

 Golem, page 270

Rimush the Golem: Rimush is a golem of few words, but it's not violent unless provoked or ordered to be so by Myth Keeper. In addition to being good with a hammer, Rimush is an artist that enjoys working in several mediums. It answers basic questions regarding its function in the Mouth of Swords but won't tell characters where any particular treasures are located. If asked about the drawing on the workbench, it identifies the sketch as "the Dustman." On the topic of the Dustman, the otherwise terse Rimush gives the following answers to questions, which are true as far as it knows:

• "The Dustman stores special treasures in the Mouth of Swords. But he is a Stranger, not of Ardeyn, and I hate him."

• "The Dustman only visited a few times. The very first time, he was with a qephilim woman with bright gold mythlight. She never came again. I never found out her name." (In fact, this was Uentaru, translated into an Ardeyn form.)

• "The Dustman visited four times that I know of. He hasn't been here in months."

• "If Myth Keeper didn't command me otherwise, I would kill the Dustman. I have saved a special device of ultimate sorcery that I would use to strike him down." (The device is a level 10 Stranger-slaying ray emitter.)

• "If you swear on the Maker to kill the Dustman, I'll give into your hands the device, since I may not use it myself." (If the PCs swear, Rimush is as good as its word.)

Workbench: Beneath the heaped, rusted swords (about thirteen or so), a large piece of parchment is visible. The parchment contains a drawing of some sort, but the swords obscure it until they are moved aside.

Pails: Three pails hold different grades of polishing sand, one pail is half filled with bolts used to secure swords to the exterior of the complex, and one pail is filled with inks and quills.

Drawing: This is a drawing of the Dustman, expertly rendered but smudged by sword rust. Rimush made it because he distrusts the Stranger.

Clay Figures: The receipts that Myth Keeper gives to depositors are in the form of tiny clay figures made by Rimush. None of those on the second workbench have yet been allocated.

RAY EMITTER (STRANGER SLAYING)

Level: 1d6 + 4
Earth: Handheld device
Ardeyn: Wand
Ruk: Shoulder-mounted module
Effect: Allows the user to project a ray up to 200 feet (61 m) that deals damage equal to the cypher level to the target. If the target is a native of the Strange itself, the difficulty of the attack roll is decreased by two steps, and the damage equals double the cypher level.

22. Exacting Shrine of Law

read aloud

Gold tiles with black highlights on the floor spiral out from the fixed statue of a female qephilim in ornate magisterial robes reading from an unfurled scroll so long that the end winds about her legs. The sculpture captures intelligence, unwavering authority, and easy assurance.

If approached, the statue animates just enough to ask the PCs to recite seven acts against Ardeyn's rules that are considered sins. If a PC answers correctly, the door to room 23 is unlocked.

Reciting the seven sins is something that Ardeyn natives or a PC trained in Ardeyn lore can attempt as a difficulty 2 Intellect-based task, one task per sin recalled. A player might also try his luck at naming the seven sins; approximate answers are accepted. However, each incorrect answer requires the answerer to succeed on an Intellect defense roll or take 3 points of damage to his Intellect Pool (ignores Armor). If three sins are described incorrectly before all seven are described correctly, a shrieking alarm sounds, and Myth Keeper and Rimush respond if they are able to do so.

23. Cold Treasure

The iron door connecting this room to room 22 is normally locked with a level 7 mechanism. If picked or opened by reciting the seven sins in room 22, the door remains unlocked for up to an hour before swinging closed and locking once more.

read aloud

Frost rimes this chamber, including three large chests along the north wall. A sword in a bright blue scabbard seems frozen to the wall over the chests.

The chests are locked (level 4 mechanism) but not otherwise protected. The first chest is the size of a person, the second is small enough to be picked up in one hand, and the third splits the difference.

Chest 1: Packed in sawdust is a fabulous feathered dragon marionette made of Marhaban silk (worth 500 crowns).

Chest 2: Packed in sawdust is a leather pouch containing three tiny clay pots stoppered with wax. Each pot holds one dose of spiral dust.

Seven Sins of Ardeyn

COMMERCE. Accumulation of obscene levels of wealth in the face of poverty

DEATH. Murder

DESIRE. Give a Stranger or Lotanist access to Ardeyn (usually because of lust or greed)

LAW. Theft of another's livelihood

LORE. Lies meant to harm another

SILENCE. Failure to aid another when it is within your power to help

WAR. Cowardice that betrays a trust

Chest 3: Packed in sawdust is one of Donna Ilsa's kidnapped eggs.

Sword in Blue Scabbard: The source of the cold in the room is an artifact frozen onto the wall. The artifact comes off with a sturdy tug (and the chill in the room immediately begins to dissipate). The artifact is a level 4 soul sword that deals an extra 4 points of damage per hit from a burst of freezing cold; depletion: 1–3 on 1d100. Though a PC wielder might be able to ascertain the foregoing by reading the bone-white runes on the blade, what's not revealed is that this is one of the cursed varieties of soul sword. When it is depleted, it requires another soul to take the place of the one previously bound to the blade. This means the current wielder's soul is forfeit unless she kills the nearest sentient creature to serve as the replacement soul.

24. Secret Chamber

The secret door leading to this chamber is well hidden and securely locked with a level 8 mechanism. Myth Keeper usually becomes fully insubstantial to access the chamber. This secret room is where the wrath lord stores the pay it receives from depositors. The room currently holds several thousand golden crowns, packed 500 to a chest.

By the end of this chapter, if the PCs have acquired some or all of the kidnapped eggs, they can return to Crow Hollow; see Returning Donna Ilsa's Eggs (page 46). Ilsa rewards the characters by telling them where her spiral dust supplier operates. However, before the PCs can take on that challenge, they're likely to be caught up in the events of Intermission 2 (page 27).

Soul weapon, page 188

Experience Point Awards: *For each of Ilsa's eggs they recover, the PCs gain 1 XP each. Defeating Myth Keeper permanently is worth 2 XP for each PC. Recovering the Stranger-slaying cypher from Rimush is worth 1 XP for each PC. These awards are in addition to any XP earned for recovering artifacts or by other means.*

Spiral Dust Effects, page 36

WHOLE BODY GRAFTS

This adventure is part of the main arc of The Dark Spiral *and is appropriate for PCs who have learned that Whole Body Grafts in Ruk is the ultimate supplier of spiral dust. As a stand-alone scenario, "Whole Body Grafts" introduces the characters to Ruk and its particular oddities, including the prolific body modification in the recursion. The PCs can also put a real end to the deadly spiral dust trade.*

BACKGROUND

Ruk operates under the law of Mad Science, and one of its specialties is body modification. One of the most expensive premier shops—Whole Body Grafts—is actually the front for spiral dust production, headed up by an entity called the Dustman. The Dustman was enjoying reasonable spread of his product, but when Uentaru approached him with a deal for increasing distribution greatly on Earth, he couldn't say no.

SYNOPSIS

PCs who investigate Whole Body Grafts discover that, for all its defenses and intrigues, it's just a front. The real source of spiral dust lies in the guts of an entity of the Strange called Nakarand, a place of true horror where all spiral dust addicts go to die and catalyze the next "crop" of the drug. If Uentaru is aiding the PCs during this part of the adventure, she endears herself to them at some point, only to make her inevitable betrayal sting all the more.

From Nakarand captives or possibly from the Dustman himself, the PCs learn that Uentaru helped the Dustman distribute spiral dust across Earth. Why? Because having more quickened people on Earth will empower the Aleph component hidden in the planet's crust. The Aleph component could then be used to recreate Uentaru's vanished homeworld, despite the fact that doing so would likely destroy the Earth and all the recursions around it. Unfortunately, events have already taken place at the center of the Earth, so it might be too late to stop her plan (or so the PCs are led to believe).

GETTING THE PCs INVOLVED

If the PCs are Estate operatives, the most straightforward way to bring them into this part of the adventure is by having the organization direct them to Ruk after they learn the name of Donna Ilsa's supplier. If that doesn't work out, try the following option.

Non-Estate PCs: A Quiet Cabal NPC agent approaches the PCs in Ruk and explains that she is preparing to storm a place called Whole Body Grafts because she suspects it's a front for dangerous interaction with entities from the Strange. There's also a reward in it for the characters (1,000 bits per PC and the gratitude of the Quiet Cabal).

MODIFYING FOR DIFFERENT TIERS

For each tier that the characters' average tier is above 1, add one more venom trooper to encounters that contain them.

If the PCs are third-tier characters or higher, increase the level of all creatures encountered by 3. See Modifying a Creature's Level for additional guidance.

If the PCs are tier 2 or lower, decrease the level of the Vengeance-class battle chrysalid, the Dustman, and Uentaru by 2.

RUK

Whole Body Grafts does business in the recursion of Ruk, so the PCs must translate there before they can shut down the spiral dust trade for good. Ruk is a land of amazing technology, miracles of biological enhancement, and feuds that have burned since before humanity evolved. *The Strange* corebook contains a complete description.

TRANSLATING TO RUK

PCs can use their type abilities to translate to Ruk. If any PC has previously traveled to the recursion, that character can initiate the translation. If no one has previously visited, PCs working for the Estate received special training that includes knowledge of three

Modifying a Creature's Level, page 16

Ruk, page 190

What a Recursor Knows About Ruk, page 190

Harmonious, page 196

All Song communal, page 198

LeRoy Cain, page 18

Inim-shara: level 4, level 5 for all tasks related to commerce

Don Wyclef, page 44

specific, related pieces of information about Ruk, which provide the impetus for the translation trance. Alternatively, the PCs might find some other way to get to Ruk.

When the PCs translate, the process imprints on them the tidbits of knowledge that a recursor knows about Ruk, if they didn't already know those things thanks to their training.

Arriving in Ruk via Translation: The default location for first-time translators to Ruk is in a wide public lobby of Harmonious, the Glistening City. A PC who has previously visited and initiated the translation appears with her group wherever she last left.

Uentaru in Ruk: If Uentaru meets the PCs in Ruk after they arrive, or if she accompanies them during their translation, she wears her golden armor and gains access to her starshine lance, as described in her full stats on page 81.

Harmonious Public Lobby: The lobby is an apparently open-air platform secured by organimer trusses between several tower structures. The platform streams with all manner of people sporting body modifications of every kind, some of them extreme. Gene-engineered pets, cybernetic couriers, and tiny robots are also present, moving between and

above the press of humanity. At the center of the platform, a public All Song communal is thick with people standing, sitting, and even lying spread-eagled, their eyes closed and their umbilicals plugged into the All Song.

Finding Whole Body Grafts: The PCs can explore Harmonious (as presented in the corebook) as they wish. When they're ready to visit Whole Body Grafts, finding it is as easy as plugging an umbilical into a nearby communal. The All Song provides location, directions, and the basic information given below under "Whole Body Grafts."

Spiral Dust Trade in Ruk: Determined PCs can find spiral dust being sold by small-time dealers (akin to LeRoy Cain). In Ruk, spiral dust isn't illegal, though it probably would be if the long-term effects of the drug were known. The All Song provides the name of a dealer (Inim-shara) who lives in the Shadowed City. If the PCs approach him, they can eventually convince him to give up the name of his supplier: Don Wyclef in Crow Hollow. (Whole Body Grafts does no spiral dust business directly in Ruk; the spiral dust created in Nakarand moves by direct translation to Beak Mafia family mansions in Crow Hollow.)

WHOLE BODY GRAFTS

PCs can learn a lot about Whole Body Grafts simply by asking the All Song. The All Song answers all queries with an overwhelming sensory dump that includes text, audio, visual, sensation, and smell.

Map: Refer to the Semerimis Tower map while PCs investigate the showroom, the surgical theaters, the research and development area, and the roof. Refer to the Nakarand map (page 75) when they venture onto the combined floors housing the massive living organism.

Location and Information: Whole Body Grafts occupies the uppermost ten levels of the Semerimis Tower, one of the twenty largest towers in Harmonious, with two hundred floors plus the roof level (floor 201). Whole Body Grafts has a public showroom on the lowest level of those it owns, occupying floors 191 and 192. Its "safe and sanitary" surgical theaters, located on floors 193 and 194, are by appointment only. The research and development labs are on the levels above the surgical theaters, floors 195 and 196. Publicly available information doesn't describe what might lie on floors 197 to 200.

A PC who succeeds on a difficulty 5 Intellect-based task learns that Whole Body Grafts is associated with the faction Zal but is more like a wholly owned subsidiary. As with many Zal facilities, access between secure areas is granted only to those who have special color-coded rings, or visitors who accompany employees with rings. White rings are least secure, and red are the most. Many Zal employees have white rings, but only a trusted few wear the red.

A successful difficulty 6 Intellect-based roll uncovers the principal owner of Whole Body Grafts: Ur-dust. No other information regarding Ur-dust is easily accessible via the All Song.

Looking for Whole Body Grafts via the All Song also floods the inquirer with advertisements from similar shops describing their wares and philosophy, as encapsulated in Body Modification Is for Everyone, a representative ad.

SHOWROOM

Gaining entry to the showroom is as simple as taking a lift from the base of Semerimis Tower or flying (through personal means, a flying rickshaw, and so on) into the aerial garage on floors 189 and 190. One main entrance to the

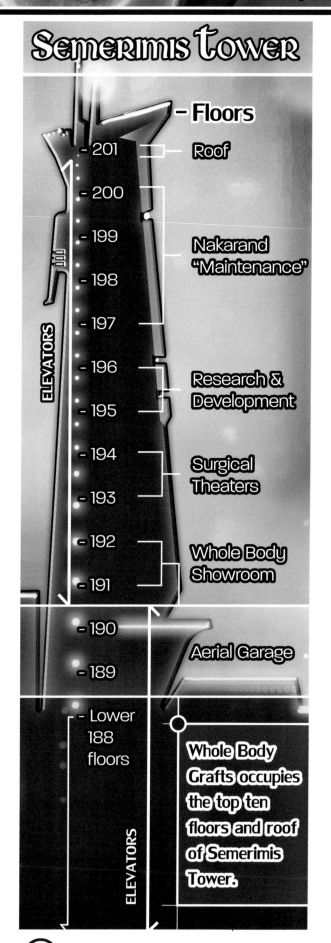

Semerimis Tower

— Floors
- 201 — Roof
- 200
- 199 — Nakarand "Maintenance"
- 198
- 197
- 196 — Research & Development
- 195
- 194 — Surgical Theaters
- 193
- 192 — Whole Body Showroom
- 191
- 190 — Aerial Garage
- 189
- Lower 188 floors

ELEVATORS

Whole Body Grafts occupies the top ten floors and roof of Semerimis Tower.

showroom channels visitors who arrive from the tower lift or aerial garage.

read aloud

This glittering showroom features several dozen amazing humanoid forms, each on a pedestal and the focus of brilliant light beams. The forms are fabulous both in their number and their elaboration. Some of the standouts include a man with elaborately streaked lavender skin sporting breathtaking musculature, a woman with beautifully textured black-and-white skin who has three arms and two heads (neither of which has hair), and a slight humanoid with blue and red skin whose unfurled wingspan covers a portion of the ceiling overhead. Customers walk among the displays, talking to sales associates about the grafts they'd like for themselves.

The showroom is open around the clock. The easiest way for the PCs to get access to the next higher section of the building is to buy a modification and schedule a procedure. However, they can also attempt to steal an access ring from an associate, hack the elevators, or use some other method.

General Security: Visible security includes seven venom troopers: three by the main entrance and two on either side of the bank of elevators that lead up to the surgical theaters. If a fight breaks out in the showroom, the venom troopers call for backup, and six more appear through the main entrance after a couple of rounds, having come up from below. Security Chief Mu-dagan also responds to any trouble.

Exits: The showroom has a few exits (besides the main entrance that leads up from the lower lifts and the aerial garage). These lead to offices, restrooms, and maintenance spaces. The central pillar in the showroom also hosts a set of matching elevators.

Elevators: Both elevators have an identical interior, which includes a touchscreen panel on the wall that displays a palm. If someone wearing an employee's ceramic ring presses her palm to the print, the elevator rises, granting access to the associated levels:

• *White ring:* the showroom and the surgical theaters.
• *Green ring:* the showroom, the surgical theaters, R&D, and the roof.
• *Red ring:* all levels, including maintenance. If the PCs enter the elevator without a

clearance ring or fail to take control of it, the elevator drops to the showroom level regardless of what they select.

A PC who tries to hack or otherwise override an elevator finds that accessing the surgical theaters is a difficulty 5 Intellect task, accessing R&D and the roof is a difficulty 6 Intellect-based task, and accessing the maintenance levels (which are actually Nakarand) is a difficulty 7 Intellect-based task.

Sales Associates: At any given time, ten sales associates in elegant white robes walk the floor, engaging the 2d6 customers browsing the wares. See the sidebar titled "PCs Buying Grafts."

Sales associates on the showroom floor don't know anything about the Dustman, spiral dust, or Nakarand. If quizzed by the PCs, the best a sales associate can do is say, "Do you mean Ur-dust? He doesn't take appointments. In fact, I've never seen him." If a PC has a lot of questions about the science behind grafts, a sales associate might suggest that the character talk with one of the chief researchers on the R&D level, but to do so, they'd need an appointment and a good reason for a researcher to give up her time. PCs who provide such a pretext can be chaperoned up to the R&D floor within the hour.

The sales associates are not heroes, and, if threatened, they give up their white rings that grant elevator access.

In any event, if the PCs press about the Dustman (or Ur-dust), start a fight, or otherwise seem to be trouble, Security Chief Mu-dagan is summoned. He always keeps an eye on what's happening throughout Whole Body Grafts using hidden cameras that feed

Venom trooper, page 300

Sales associate: level 3, level 5 for all tasks related to sales; wears white ring

Customer: level 2

Mu-dagan: level 5; Armor 3 (hidden carapace graft); attacks two targets in long range as a single action with needler for 5 points of damage per shot; wears red ring

Graft technician: level 3, level 5 for all tasks related to medical procedures; wears green ring

BODY MODIFICATION IS FOR EVERYONE!

YOUR BODY is a canvas, a space to mix and match physical and philosophical elements that define who or what you want to be. We provide surgical body modifications and grafts for spiritual, decorative, and personal protection purposes. The pain of the modification is part of your spiritual journey to a new you, so don't let that deter you. Explore something as simple as a body piercing or as extreme as an entirely new dermal layer to achieve a unique *new* look.

to his office in one of the side rooms on this floor.

Security Chief Mu-dagan: Dressed in white robes with red trim (and wearing a red ring), Mu-dagan plays the part of the sincere company manager who makes things right for customers who feel they've been wronged. If he identifies the PCs as troublemakers, he tries to defray a tense situation by offering free sessions for each character in one of the "safe and sanitary" surgical theaters. "If you will just follow me?"

Mu-dagan's red ring offers access to all the levels above 190, including the maintenance levels, where Nakarand is hosted.

If Mu-dagan believes the PCs are ordinary troublemakers, he keeps his word about the complimentary sessions, in which each character can receive a standard graft or body modification of her choice. However, if he has reason to believe that the PCs know about the Dustman or the spiral dust production on floors 197 to 200, he programs the surgical theater for a mishap.

Of course, if the PCs offer direct physical violence, Mu-dagan fights back, summoning the seven visible venom troopers (who are followed by an additional six who storm up from the aerial garage). Troopers on other levels (as described below) go on alert, and the PCs find it more difficult to move unseen or under the guise of people that belong.

SURGICAL THEATERS

Two large floors of Semerimis Tower are given over to performing the procedures. A maze of hallways leads away from the waiting room, connecting to twenty surgical theaters, three recovery rooms, an impressively large tissue bank, and staff lounges. If the PCs are interested in visiting any of these chambers, glowing, labeled lines on the floor lead them wherever they'd like to go on the level.

In addition to the personnel described below, twelve venom troopers patrol the hallways in case someone wakes up with a new graft and becomes dangerous.

WAITING ROOM

PCs who get off the elevators on either of the two surgical theater floors appear in a waiting room where 1d6 customers wait for procedures.

Graft Technicians: The waiting room also usually hosts 1d6 graft technicians in white

PCS BUYING GRAFTS

A sales associate can explain to curious PCs that Whole Body Grafts, despite the name, also offers a host of lesser modifications and grafts, in addition to the attention-getting "whole body" options on display. A PC who makes use of the services offered—whether standard graft, body modification, or whole body graft—retains that mod each time he translates back to Ruk.

Standard Grafts: The shop will create a custom graft from almost any piece of Ruk equipment listed in the corebook (page 91) for ten times the listed price. This does not apply to armor. If a PC wants a carapace graft, for instance, he actually wants a whole body graft.

The item grafted becomes part of the PC's body as if it were a natural limb. Such a graft can be "folded" away when it would be inconvenient, or instantly deployed when the PC wants to use it. Whole Body Grafts works with the customer to determine the form of the graft, based on the equipment chosen. For instance, if a PC wants a binoculars graft, the price is 100 bits and the procedure takes an hour in a surgical theater. When the PC emerges, he might have a biomechanical fleshy "hood" he can lower over his eyes to see farther when needed, or nictitating "binocular membranes" he can blink into play.

Body Modifications: The shop is also happy to help clients artistically restyle their bodies and offers a complimentary consultation along with any paid modification. Prices run from 10 to 200 bits for the modification services.

Services include permanent "shaped" holes (such as heart, diamond, or circle) through nonvital limbs, limb extension, implants (3D art implants, genital beading, transdermal implants, silicone injection, and more), castration, corsetry, tongue splitting, scarification, tooth art, facial sculpture, fingernail mods, urethral reroutes, and amputations.

Piercing Services: 10 bits per piercing, plus the cost of the ring, stud, or other piercing item (which runs from 10 to 100 bits). Types of piercings offered include bridge (horizontal piercing through the bridge of the nose), cheek, chin, custom (something unusual), daith (inner ear cartilage piercing), eyebrow, genital (ampallang or Christina), hand web (piercing in the finger webbing), knuckle (surface piercing between the knuckles on the top of the hand), labret (lower lip piercing), Madison (surface piercing at base of neck), nape (back of neck piercing), navel, nipple, nostril, tongue, and wrist.

Whole Body Grafts: A whole body graft is a more extreme version of a standard graft, as it essentially involves peeling away the client's skin and replacing it with something else. For example, a PC can get a whole body graft of Ruk armor (for ten times the listed price of each armor set). Doing so allows a PC to "fold" the armor away when it's not in use, even a carapace. The armor drapes like a cape or another dramatic, flaring shape behind the character. PCs can also request more extreme body replacements. The GM and player should work together to come up with something that satisfies both.

robes with blue trim. The graft technicians have similar knowledge about spiral dust and the Dustman as the sales associates do (none), and they summon Mu-dagan if they see PCs wandering the area without an appointment or a chaperone with the proper ring clearance. Each graft technician wears a green ring, which grants access to the showroom, the surgical theaters, research and development, and the roof.

Elevators: These are the same as described for the elevators in the showroom, requiring the same ring-clearances to function.

SURGICAL THEATERS

A red light outside a closed door means that theater is occupied, and the door won't open unless hacked or forced (the doors are level 5 mechanisms). A green light outside a closed door means that theater is unoccupied, and the door opens to a touch. About half of the twenty surgical theaters are occupied at any given time.

read aloud

A metallic chair with numerous metallic clamps is nestled in the center of a nightmare sphere of mechanical arms. They are customized for slicing, lasering, sawing, injecting, suturing, and less obvious methods for modifying the flesh of whoever straps in.

If a PC wants a graft or modification, she must sit in the chair. An attending graft technician will instruct the mechanism through an umbilical just outside the door.

Each procedure normally lasts one hour whether it's successful or not. Technicians rarely fail to program a surgical theater correctly. However, if a PC attempts to instruct the surgical theater to perform a procedure, she must succeed on a difficulty 4 Intellect-based task or suffer a mishap (for added tension, don't ask her to roll until after the procedure is finished). If Mu-dagan has lured the PCs to a surgical theater because he suspects they are saboteurs, he automatically triggers a mishap with the mechanism.

Surgical Theater Mishap: When a mishap occurs, roll on the following table and apply the result. If the PC gains one or more deformities, roll on the Harmful Mutations table in the corebook (page 240). All mishap results can be reversed with another session

in a surgical theater with a competent programmer setting up the procedure.

1	The PC descends one step on the damage track; normal recovery fails to erase step damage until 24 hours have passed.
2	The PC slips into a coma. Once a day, she can attempt a difficulty 5 Might-based roll to rouse herself.
3	The PC gains one deformity.
4	The PC gains two deformities.
5	he PC gains three deformities.
6	The PC's head is sutured onto a small animal that resembles a hairless dog, and her body is stored in the tissue bank.

OTHER ROOMS

The other chambers on these levels (staff lounges, tissue banks, recovery rooms, and so on) are unlikely to come into play during the course of this adventure, but feel free to detail them as needed.

RESEARCH AND DEVELOPMENT

Two large floors of Semerimis Tower are given over to research on improving the services offered by Whole Body Grafts.

A maze of hallways leads away from the R&D lobby checkpoint, connecting to a dizzying array of labs that conduct research through a variety of analytical methods using impressively advanced equipment. The R&D floors also host rooms for cold storage, experimental surgical theaters, chemical storage, medical-grade radioactive isotope storage, and so on.

In addition to the personnel described below, twelve venom troopers patrol the hallways, on alert against rival faction spies attempting industrial espionage (or other disruptions).

R&D LOBBY

PCs who get off the elevators on either of the two research and development floors appear in a lobby that has comfortable seating, refreshments, and a counter behind which a few R&D associates stand ready to help researchers or authorized guests.

Elevators: These are the same as described for the elevators in the showroom, requiring the same ring-clearances to function.

R&D Associates: R&D associates wear white robes with green trim. They have similar knowledge about spiral dust and the Dustman as the sales associates do (none), and they summon Mu-dagan if they see PCs wandering

R&D researcher: level 3, level 4 for all tasks related to molecular, cellular, and biological research; wears green ring

Chief R&D researcher: level 3, level 6 for all tasks related to molecular, cellular, and biological research; wears red ring

R&D associate: level 3, level 4 for all tasks related to research protocol; wears green ring

the area without an appointment or a chaperone with the proper ring clearance. Each R&D associate wears a green ring, which grants access to the showroom, the surgical theaters, research and development, and the roof.

If PCs ask about the maintenance floors, the associates indicate that only red-ring clearance grants such access, and that only Mu-dagan, Ur-dust, and a handful of the fifty or so researchers who work in R&D have red rings. The associates would be happy to summon Mu-dagan or, if the PCs have somehow fast-talked their way to this floor without arousing suspicion, one of the R&D researchers with a red ring.

Chief R&D Researchers: There are four chief researchers with red rings: Iphur-kishi, Pra-qatum, Ipqu-adad, and Dram-shara (although Dram-shara went missing a few days ago; see area 8 of Nakarand). If one of them is summoned by an R&D associate or if the PCs find one in the array of labs on the R&D levels, characters who are skilled at persuasion can learn more about what's going on, at least as far as the scientists understand it:

• "Spiral dust? Never heard of it." (If told about spiral dust, most R&D researchers ask for a sample so they can run tests, but they don't react in outrage.)

• "Ur-dust isn't a native of Ruk; he's a native of the Strange. He's the one who gave us Nakarand. We only see him when he's tending the Nakarand Project on the maintenance levels."

• "The Nakarand Project is named for Nakarand itself. It's a living mass of immense size with unexplainable abilities and powers. It's some kind of chimera of strange genes and enzymes. We take samples from it regularly and use them as the basis of our research. We've developed more than one graft improvement from studying the creature."

• "In return for tissue samples, we house Nakarand and supply cloned venom workers to Ur-dust when he asks. We have clone banks set up on the maintenance levels."

• "The Nakarand Project is a Zal trade secret, as I'm sure you can appreciate. Blabbing about trade secrets to other factions is strictly prohibited by factol decree, so don't go spreading what we've told you, unless you're looking forward to a visit by a troop of Myriand."

• "We feed clone-grown laborers to Nakarand, but that's not my area. You'd have to talk to Bel-temar up in Maintenance."

Myriand, page 198

Bel-temar, page 74

OTHER ROOMS

The other chambers on these levels (analytical labs, cold storage rooms, experimental surgical theaters, chemical storage rooms, medical-grade radioactive isotope storage vaults, and so on) are unlikely to come into play during the course of this adventure, but feel free to detail them as needed.

A total of about ten R&D associates (whose white robes have one green stripe) and fifty R&D researchers (whose white robes have two green stripes) can be found throughout the section, attending to their experiments during regular shift hours.

ROOF

Semerimis Tower's "floor 201" is the roof, which, despite its apparent openness, is defended against unscheduled landings. In addition to the roof security, the area hosts a large power station and a hangar with flying craft in case evacuation is needed.

Elevators: These are the same as described for the elevators in the showroom, requiring the same ring-clearances to function.

Roof Security: Roof security includes two autonomous gun turrets and a company of twelve venom troopers stationed in a permanent structure backed up to the power station. The turrets are positioned so that between them, they cover the entire roof. Avoiding the attention of the venom troopers and the turrets is a difficulty 5 Speed-based task that must be performed each minute an infiltrator remains active on the roof.

If one autonomous turret and/or half the venom troopers are defeated in combat, the Vengeance-class battle chrysalid is summoned from the hangar.

Power Station: A massive structure on the roof provides power that runs Semerimis Tower's elevators, lights, research equipment, air circulation stations, and other mechanisms. Accessing the power station and selectively turning off and on subsystems requires several minutes of uninterrupted concentration and a successful difficulty 5 Intellect-based roll for each subsystem cracked. A failed attempt is usually good for summoning more security.

Hangar: The hangar (locked with a level 5 mechanism) houses a vehicle akin to a private jet, except the wings are far stubbier than one would expect on Earth, and flying it is much easier, requiring a green or red clearance ring and a difficulty 3 Intellect-based roll for standard maneuvers.

The hangar also contains an inactive Vengeance-class battle chrysalid in standby mode. If the PCs are subtle, they can avoid triggering its activation. Remember to reduce the chrysalid's level as described at the beginning of this chapter if the PCs are tier 2 or lower.

Uentaru: If Uentaru is with the PCs or the characters summon her, she goes above and beyond to gain their trust by apparently putting her life on the line against the battle chrysalid. She tells the PCs that she'll hold the thing off while they get to the elevators. (Later, she catches up with them before they enter Nakarand or joins them after they've already entered.)

Autonomous gun turret: level 3; health 12; fixed to roof; long-range projectile attack that inflicts 4 points of damage

GM Intrusion: *Consider presenting the Vengeance-class battle chrysalid encounter as a group GM intrusion (see page 341 of The Strange corebook for more information).*

VENGEANCE-CLASS BATTLE CHRYSALID 7 (21)

A chrysalid is an engineered body in Ruk made to fulfill a purpose. Battle chrysalides, for instance, are made for conflict. Chrysalides come into being after normal Rukians receive expensive modifications that give access to a chrysalid form (such as is the case for a Myriand or a PC who Metamorphosizes). However, some modifications are so extreme that certain classes of chrysalid do not allow regression back to normal—at least, not without the intervention of a surgical procedure, such as is the case with a Vengeance-class battle chrysalid.

These battle chrysalides control an amazing amount of firepower, but in return, they give up a bit of autonomy. Designated commanders can upload their orders to the chrysalid via umbilical link. Though this interface allows a chrysalid's firepower to remain under control, it also introduces a vulnerability; see Interaction.

Motive: Follow programming of battle commander

Environment (Ruk | Mad Science): Anywhere

Health: 21

Damage Inflicted: 10 points

Armor: 3

Movement: Short when walking or flying

Modifications: Speed defense as level 5 due to size.

Combat: A Vengeance-class battle chrysalid can make a single attack with a fist or a shoulder-mounted laser cannon (long range) for 10 points of damage. It can instead attack two different foes as a single action, inflicting 8 points of damage with

both attacks (fists or long-range laser cannons).

Once every other round, a Vengeance-class battle chrysalid can fire a grenade at a target or area within long range that explodes in an immediate radius for 8 points of damage. Creatures that succeed on a Speed defense roll still take 1 point of damage from shrapnel.

A Vengeance-class battle chrysalid regenerates 1 point of health per round while its health is above 0.

Interaction: A Vengeance-class battle chrysalid specifies its current duties if queried, but otherwise it doesn't interact. However, if a PC is able to attach her umbilical to the port on the back of the chrysalid's "neck," she can attempt to compromise its orders. Doing so is a multistep process, first requiring a difficulty 5 Speed or Might defense roll each round to remain clinging to the bucking chrysalid's back, and then requiring two difficulty 5 Intellect-based rolls, one per round. The first successful reprogramming roll modifies the chrysalid's actions and defenses by two steps to its detriment, and the second successful roll puts the chrysalid in standby mode.

Use: Any time the GM needs an extremely potent guardian for an area in Ruk, a Vengeance-class battle chrysalid is a good choice.

Loot: PCs who investigate an inert Vengeance-class battle chrysalid discover that 1d6 cyphers have been worked into the mechanism and can be salvaged with a successful difficulty 3 Intellect-based task.

NAKARAND
Floors 197 to 200 of Semerimis Tower host Nakarand, though most employees of Whole Body Grafts don't know that. Those who have heard the term don't know that Nakarand is an entity originally native to the Strange that serves as the ultimate source of spiral dust.

1. MAINTENANCE LOBBY ELEVATORS
These elevators are the same as described for the elevators in the showroom, requiring the same ring-clearances to function or hacking skills to override. One thing that becomes apparent only after the fact is that the elevators only go to floor 199, red ring or not—floors 197 through 200 apparently belong to one "mega" floor.

Vengeance-class battle chrysalides are fashioned of normal Rukians, as opposed to venom troopers, which are synthesized entities.

GM Intrusion: *The character is knocked down and disarmed by the chrysalid, which offers the PC a chance to surrender.*

2. Maintenance Lobby

Venom worker: level 1; no attacks

Bel-temar: level 3, level 6 for all tasks related to molecular, cellular, and biological research; wears red ring

read aloud

This wide room is clean but smells strongly of brine, like the sea. Several comfortable chairs and lounges are cluttered near the elevators, but the middle of the large chamber is bare. A counter stands opposite the elevators, helpfully labeled "Maintenance Desk." Three people in maintenance onesies work the desk.

Assuming that Whole Body Grafts hasn't gone on alert because of a fight involving the PCs within the previous few hours, characters who arrive on the elevator don't initially raise the suspicions of the maintenance desk staff. Even so, getting past the staff without triggering countermeasures is tricky.

Maintenance desk staffer: level 3, level 6 for all tasks related to seeing through deception; wears green ring

Maintenance Desk Staff: The three people behind the counter wear grey onesies reminiscent of coveralls for laborers in many recursions and on Earth. Each wears a green ring (Mu-dagan oversees shift changes).

It's difficult to deceive the maintenance staff, and attempting to do so and failing triggers the security countermeasures. But PCs who manage it can learn everything from the staff that the chief R&D researchers know about the Nakarand Project.

Chief R&D researcher, page 71

Security Countermeasures: If the PCs arrive in this chamber with the alarm already raised or if they make the desk staff suspicious (and it's the desk staff's job to be suspicious), a 20-foot-by-20-foot (6 m by 6 m) section of the ceiling drops down. Revealed are twelve venom troopers or (if the PCs haven't yet faced the chrysalid on the roof) a Vengeance-class battle chrysalid. Use the information provided for the chrysalid attack on the roof here instead, including Uentaru's offer of aid. (Don't make the PCs fight one of these things twice; once is probably enough.)

3. Venom Clone Vats

Nakarand: level 10; health 100; Armor 10; regenerates 10 points of health per round

read aloud

Thick brownish-pink fluid swirls and bubbles inside massive transparent tanks that line the walls. Each tank is connected by tubes and cords to an associated metallic enclosure with a transparent lid, similar to a sarcophagus. Within the foggy interior of several enclosures, humanoid forms lie unmoving.

About half the vats and associated "body molds" are used to grow venom troopers (complete with armor; armament provided separately). The other half grow similar entities called venom workers that are made for labor, not defense.

Venom Vat Maintenance: A single red-ringed R&D researcher (Bel-temar) tends the vats here, and he knows the same things the chief R&D researchers know about the Nakarand Project, as well as the following:

• "We purchased these vats from Zal to create venom troopers. We modified a few to make venom workers, which do for labor what troopers do for security."

• "Almost all the venom workers grown here are destined for Nakarand. The thing eats them. Well, that's what we thought, but apparently, ingested workers survive for a time and help the Dustman accomplish something inside. We've seen the Dustman enter and leave Nakarand, and sometimes venom workers too. But more of them go in than ever come out again."

• "The Dustman needs the workers for whatever he does inside Nakarand. He lets us keep the biological samples we cull from the exterior. In return, we don't ask what goes on inside the organism, though of course we're curious."

• "Whatever need the Dustman has for venom workers, he goes through them pretty fast. We deliver a new worker about once a day."

4. Nakarand Feedway

read aloud

A sticky, brownish organism, vast and coiled, fills a multistory space hollowed inside the tower. A pier extends from the chamber entrance, protruding so that its tip is poised immediately before the organism's slowly chewing, sluglike maw. The smell of ocean brine and an underlying stink of rot are overwhelming.

Nakarand is a native of the Chaosphere, currently hosted by Ruk. Its exterior presents like a living creature of exceptional size, but Nakarand is bigger on the inside than the outside, and reality within it is subtly shifted. In some ways, the creature's interior is like a separate recursion.

Feeding Pier: About once a day, a venom clone from room 3 is escorted here by a couple of venom troopers and prodded until it stands on the pier's edge. This movement

Nakarand Map

Legend: ▮ Door · Clone Vat

Distance begins to break down ☒

N

1 · 2 · 1 · 4 · 5 · 6 · 10' · 3 · 7 · 8

rouses the massive organism, which raises its mouth to the pier and ingests whatever is there, leaving behind goo that smells of brine.

If the PCs stake out the location, they note the occasional feeding. Normally, the Dustman translates between locations, so he rarely comes and goes by way of the feeding pier. However, on any given day, there's a 1 in 20 chance that he wants something from the researchers a few floors down, and he finds it easier to "exit" Nakarand through the mouth. When that happens, it looks like the giant organism vomits him up.

PCs who stand on the edge of the pier are swallowed through the inapposite gate that serves as the living recursion's mouth, and they appear in its interior (area 5).

PCs who rain down fire and destruction on Nakarand from the pier find that the creature is incredibly hardy. However, it responds with a swallow attack (which, if successful, does no damage and deposits its victims in area 5).

5. INSIDE NAKARAND

read aloud

A sourceless, pale blue light gives everything, even your own flesh, a washed-out look. The air is thick and salty, but breathable. There is no apparent gravity, and you float in a vast, open space, bounded behind you by a wall of slowly undulating fleshy material, and stretching away in the opposite direction as if you're inside a great, living worm. Fist-sized bubbles float here and there, nodules filled with white fluid. They grow thicker as they get farther from the bounding wall of material behind you, making it difficult to see too far ahead.

Nakarand's interior is akin to a separate recursion in the sense that the laws of reality within it are altered in several immediately obvious ways. However, it's not a fully realized recursion of its own; while it's in Ruk, it's part of the recursion of Ruk.

Inconstant Space: Areas within Nakarand are larger than the exterior (and different from location to location). Outside, one map square is roughly equal to 10 feet (3 m) on a side, but in area 5, one map square is roughly equal to 100 feet (30 m) on a side.

No Gravity? At first it seems there's no gravity within Nakarand, though that's not entirely true. In fact, the inconstant space quality confers another odd property on creatures in Nakarand: while inside, they can fly at their regular movement speed. This

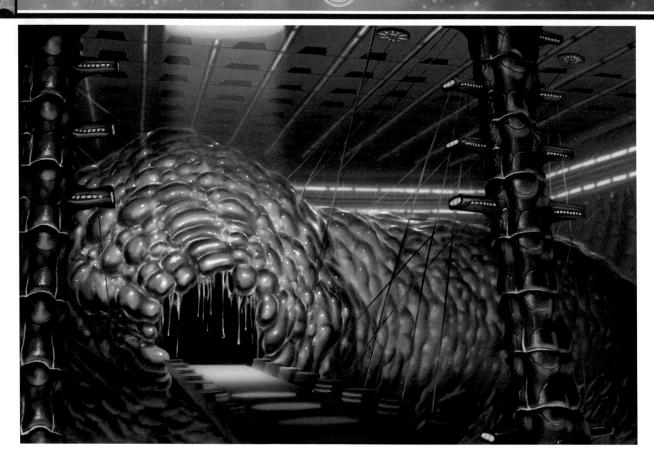

Show 'Em: Nakarand Feedway, Image J, page 95

might take the PCs a few minutes to get used to, but it doesn't ultimately penalize their actions or tasks.

Floating Spheres: The floating spheres are far enough apart in area 5 that the PCs can easily avoid them. If they investigate the spheres, each bubble has enough surface tension that it doesn't immediately pop if touched. However, a prick or slap causes a bubble to collapse, releasing a milky acid that inflicts 1 point of damage to the investigating PC. If a PC takes damage, he might notice (difficulty 3 Intellect-based check) that the burned area of his skin isn't blackened so much as "blue-ened."

The floating spheres are a side effect of Nakarand's digestion described in area 8. If the PCs spent more than four or five days inside, they'd begin to feel the same long-term lethal effects indicated for the venom workers in area 8.

Cyphers in Spheres: Because Nakarand is from the Strange, it sometimes condenses cyphers the way that a recursion does. Every so often, a pricked or burst floating sphere disgorges a randomly determined cypher along with the milky fluid. However, the more spheres that are purposefully burst searching for cyphers, the more the other spheres are

attracted to the PCs. If the characters continue to disturb the spheres after they've found several cyphers, a "bubble vortex" (see area 7) is soon created, with the PCs as the focus. Before the vortex forms, it should be obvious to the characters that their actions are creating a dangerous disturbance.

6. WAVING FRONDS

read aloud
The sides of the long, curled tube you swim down seem to constrict until it's only about 40 feet (12 m) across. Thousands of waving yellow fronds growing from the sides of the passage limit your vision to just a few paces.

Distance in this area is more like the dimensions outside of Nakarand, and each map square corresponds to 10 feet (3 m) on a side. Travelers who push deeper down Nakarand's gullet discover that distances open up again toward area 7.

Yellow Fronds of Recovery: The fronds are semi-independent organs of Nakarand involved in the entity's health and maintenance. If any creature moves near them, the fronds begin to reach for the intruder in a way that might seem threatening.

Attacks against the fronds cause them to curl away, allowing a determined PC to get through without being touched.

However, anyone who allows the fronds to pat and flicker across his body can immediately make a recovery roll without using an action, and the roll doesn't count against the daily limit of recovery rolls. The fronds confer this benefit on any given creature once per day.

7. BUBBLE EXUBERANCE

read aloud
The sides of the tube you're passing through open up somewhat, but some kind of standing-wave effect in the air disturbs the normally placidly floating bubbles ahead, churning them into a vortex that fills the tube.

The fabric of space in area 7 expands so that one map square is equal to 50 feet (15 m) on a side. Beyond area 7, distance continues to expand even further.

Bubble Vortex: A character passing through the bubble vortex is splattered with acidic bubbles and possibly gets turned around. Each time a PC makes an attempt to get through, she must succeed on a difficulty 4 Speed-based task. On a success, she makes it through but still takes 3 points of damage. On a failed roll, she takes 3 points of damage, and the vortex spins her around and spits her out the way she entered. If she wants to get through, she'll have to try again.

8. NAKARAND DIGESTION
The sides of the tube fall away in a haze of bubbles as the PCs gaze down on a truly vast area. The fabric of space in area 8 expands so that one map square is equal to about 1 mile (2 km). From a distance, the PCs get an overview of the situation:

read aloud
Hanging in the center of the space, a mottled-blue-and-white planetoid is visible. A curling spindle of Nakarand plunges down into the heart of the object, like a long straw punched into the side of a swollen and half-rotted blueberry. The tubelike spindle slowly undulates. Milky bubbles seep up through gaps and cracks in the planetoid's surface. An artificial structure forged of silvery metal is visible on the planetoid's surface near where the tube is attached.

If PCs approach (or have some kind of vision-magnifying device), they can see what's going on, though it might leave them with more questions than answers.

read aloud
The tortured texture of the planetoid resolves: it's made of people. To cover the surface of a planetoid more than a mile in radius like this one would require thousands of bodies. Milky fluid runs like veins across the entire imperfect sphere, and where the fluid runs, the bodies have become partly petrified blue sculptures. Several figures are moving around near the artificial structure, revealed as a metallic building.

The PCs have some leeway to investigate the strange tableau until the Dustman arrives to challenge their intrusion.

Massed Bodies: PCs who investigate the bodies (all without clothing or possessions) discover that though they are apparently dead, none are rotting—at least not in a normal fashion. Instead of breaking the bodies down by bacterial decay, the milky white fluid flowing across (and under) the surface is extracting soft tissue and leaving behind a bluish material that is as hard and brittle as chalk. If powdered, the material becomes spiral dust.

If the PCs don't realize the truth, the R&D researcher trapped in the artificial structure or the Dustman himself can confirm that the "mass grave" floating at Nakarand's core is composed of spiral dust addicts who have overdosed and translated here (even if they weren't technically quickened, they were while high on the drug).

Undulating Spindle Tube: The tube is something like Nakarand's proboscis. It distributes the milky white enzyme and sucks up the resultant nutritious mix, leaving behind the waste product: petrified blue bodies (solid spiral dust).

Artificial Structure: The silvery structure on the planetoid is a large metallic warehouse with an open front. It's half filled with lines of petrified bodies stacked like cordwood, several busy venom workers, and one R&D researcher in hiding.

Venom Workers and Stacked Bodies: The figures the PCs spied from afar are venom workers, many of them "blue-end" with constant exposure to the digestive enzymes. Their job is to quarry fully petrified bodies from the planetoid, bring

GM Intrusion: *A PC investigating the bodies is startled when a stiff suddenly opens his eyes and begins screaming. Jonathan Ballard (level 1) has only recently overdosed and just made the translation. If pulled free from the matrix of corpses, he survives the ordeal (though he's way out of his league).*

Venom worker: level 1; no attacks

Show 'Em: Planetoid of people, Image K, page 96

Dram-shara: level 3, level 5 for all tasks related to investigation and biological research; wears red ring

them into the warehouse, and stack them neatly. Any given venom worker lives for only five days before it succumbs to the environment, and then its body is in turn stacked by its fellows.

If the venom workers are left to their own tasks, they ignore the PCs. They're mute, so they're not a great source of direct information.

R&D Researcher: Dram-shara, the chief R&D researcher who went missing from Semerimis Tower a few days ago, is here of her own volition. Unlike her fellows, she wanted to know more about the Dustman's motivations and what was going on inside the great organism. She learned a lot more than she bargained for.

Dustman: At some point during the PCs' investigation of the planetoid, the star of the show makes his appearance. See "The Dustman Arrives."

MEETING DRAM-SHARA

If Dram-shara sees the PCs in or anywhere near the warehouse, she emerges from hiding and asks for their help in getting away. She is a bit shell-shocked and shows signs of extensive "blue-ing" because of how long she's been subjected to the environment.

She is also a great way for the PCs to get a summary of what's going on inside Nakarand. If asked, she explains about the massive tube proboscis and other things the characters have questions about.

If Dram-shara doesn't explain the workings to the PCs, the Dustman still might—at least, until Uentaru interrupts him.

• "Nakarand is an entity from the Strange. Even before Whole Body Grafts decided to secretly host it in Semerimis Tower, the creature was feeding on living things from Earth and recursions in the Shoals of Earth."

• "Nakarand has a peculiar feeding strategy. A sentient extension of the creature—an avatar called the Dustman—spreads spiral dust through various locations. Spiral dust is highly addictive, and even creatures without the spark can become partially quickened while the drug is in their system."

• "A spiral dust addict's first and last full-body translation transfers her here, where she becomes trapped and dies as the Nakarand's enzyme digests her flesh. What remains is a waste product that is converted to spiral dust by the simple application of blunt force."

• "Since I've been here, I've discovered that the Dustman shows up on an irregular schedule, and he translates out with a stack of petrified bodies, presumably delivering them to whatever distribution network he's set up." (The PCs might recall what they encountered on Earth and in Crow Hollow.)

• "Believe me: Whole Body Grafts didn't know this was happening. Thanks to the unending supply of venom workers we've sent in here, the Dustman has increased his production by a few orders of magnitude. I'm worried where it will end. It should be stopped. If you can get me out of here safely, I'll make certain that the powers that be eject Nakarand from the premises, one way or the other."

THE DUSTMAN ARRIVES

The Dustman is the intelligent, mobile avatar of Nakarand, so he knows when the PCs have entered the entity's body (which is part of him). However, he has been using his powerful translation abilities to chase down information on Uentaru. He only manages to put the last pieces of the puzzle in place after the characters (with Uentaru in tow) begin exploring Nakarand.

Traveling Dustman: The Dustman is an entity of the Strange and doesn't follow the same rules for translation that player characters do. When he translates, he can always translate to anywhere inside of Nakarand no matter where in Ruk he last translated from. He needs only a one-minute translation trance before transition. And whatever recursion the Dustman appears in, he always has the same look and the same abilities. He also has a special sense for anyone who has recently taken spiral dust and can translate to within short range of anyone "enjoying" the drug's effects, even if he hasn't previously been to the recursion in question.

read aloud

A passing shadow leaves in its wake a hooded man whose voluminous cloak is like layered shadows. The man says in a raspy voice, "Uentaru, have you delivered these intruders to my stomach so we can eliminate them together?"

The Dustman's Motivations: The Dustman is an extension of Nakarand and, as such, is most concerned about feeding, which means spreading spiral dust to create addicts. When Uentaru approached him with a plan to increase his spiral dust distribution (and thus his feeding ground), he jumped at the chance. At first, it seemed like the perfect match,

especially since the Ruk venom workers allowed so much more productivity. Nakarand vastly increased its nutritional intake, and Uentaru increased the apparent number of quickened creatures on Earth. The Dustman never really questioned why she wanted that.

But in recent months, the Dustman did begin to wonder, and he discovered that though their aims seemed aligned, the opposite was true. He learned that if Uentaru completes her plan, Earth and all the recursions in its Shoals will be destroyed. Given that Earth and its Shoals are the richest feeding ground he has ever found, the Dustman wants to prevent this outcome.

Thus, his greeting to Uentaru is meant to reveal her as a betrayer to the PCs, not an offer to join forces and kill the characters.

If given the chance, the Dustman reveals Uentaru's real plan (see below). In addition, if the PCs request it as a sign of good faith, he is willing to remove Nakarand from the tower and scale back his distribution of spiral dust on Earth, at least for a time.

When the Dustman appears and makes the announcement that reveals Uentaru as a traitor, treat it like a group GM intrusion (see page 341 of The Strange *corebook for more information).*

The Dustman knows that if he is defeated, another avatar of Nakarand will arise and take up his work. Thus, even if the PCs turn on him, he makes sure they get his entropic seed, along with an explanation of its significance. Ultimately, the Dustman won't finish off the PCs because he realizes they are his best hope of retaining his rich feeding ground.

UENTARU'S REAL PLAN

If Uentaru is present and challenged by the Dustman as described above, she suffers a moment of alarm, visible to any PCs studying her. But she quickly recovers and accuses the Dustman of trying to divide "the forces of justice" that have come to put an end to his horrifying feeding on Earth.

If the PCs quiz the Dustman further, he reveals what he has learned of Uentaru's real plan. Under other circumstances, Uentaru might reveal some or all of these points, too, but only if she believes her plan is about to succeed.

Uentaru's Real Plan, from the Dustman's Point of View:

• "I have watched Uentaru since she and I began working together to spread spiral dust. I've recently learned her real plan."

• "After thousands of years of searching the Strange network, Uentaru found Earth—and more important, the Aleph component buried in the mantle beneath the crust. The Aleph component is a piece of the ancient mechanism that first created the Strange billions of years ago. The component is the reason Earth is special and hosts so many quickened creatures and recursions. Its impact with your proto-planet created the Earth's moon, so it is not small or delicate."

• "Uentaru wants to use the power of the buried Aleph component to revive a recursion of her destroyed homeworld. This requires that the component be fully woken by setting up a planetwide resonance with quickened minds. Earth and its recursions don't possess nearly enough quickened to create such an effect. However, minds become briefly quickened while affected by the fertilizer of Nakarand—the spiral dust. Not knowing her ultimate purpose, I became her ally and

magnified the number of quickened on Earth and in its Shoals a thousandfold or more."

• "The Aleph component is waking. I don't know if it will give Uentaru the mastery over reality she desires or the ability to resurrect her world, Mycaeum. But I know one thing. When it fully wakes and is triggered to do her bidding, the Earth and its recursions will shatter."

• "I propose a new alliance: you and I against Uentaru. I don't want Earth and its recursions to be destroyed. If you or someone in your organization can reach the Aleph component buried beneath the Earth's mantle, I have something that might shut it down, though I fear it has already gone past the point of no return." (He's referring to his entropic seed, noted in the Dustman's equipment.)

It's up to the PCs to decide whether they believe the Dustman or Uentaru. Both deserve to be stopped. At some point during the course of your game, conflict between the characters, the Dustman, and Uentaru is inevitable (whether the PCs begin it or Uentaru lashes out against the "lying" Dustman). It's possible that conflict breaks out even before the Dustman reveals her true plan. However, if he and the PCs defeat her, he still offers them an alliance. He would prefer to accompany them to the Aleph component, but he understands if they'd rather not allow a mass-murdering creature from the Strange as a member of their group.

UENTARU, CHAOS TEMPLAR 6 (18)

Over centuries of existence, the extraterrestrial humanoid Uentaru has gathered knowledge of the Strange, power from cyphers, and reality and entropic seeds, and she has mastered the use of an artifact called the starshine lance, a beam weapon that fires coherent space-time. She founded the Chaos Templars, a group of fellow survivors drawn from across the universe of shattered prime worlds who pledged to find methods of killing planetovores. However, Uentaru's secret quest is to find some way to redeem her destroyed homeworld.

Like all Chaos Templars, Uentaru sometimes commits random acts of kindness, though other times she ignores those in need. She might seem understandable at times, but she and every Chaos Templar is alien and just as often comes across as inscrutable. In the end, she cares far more for a chance to revive her homeworld than she does for Earth or any other living creature.

Motive: Redeem her destroyed homeworld

Environment (the Strange | Mad Science): Anywhere

Health: 27

Damage Inflicted: 6 points

Armor: 2

Movement: Short

Modifications: Speed defense as level 7 due to golden armor; all tasks involving deception as level 8.

Combat: Uentaru's armored fist or foot is a melee weapon in its own right, but her most impressive weapon is her starshine lance. The lance is a ranged weapon that fires coherent space-time at targets within immediate range of each other and within Uentaru's direct line of sight, up to 2 miles (3 km) away. When she focuses the beam on one foe, the attack ignores Armor. When she widens the aperture so that an attack targets several creatures at once (essentially, as many creatures as she can see at the same time within immediate range of each other), the attack does not ignore Armor.

During any round in which Uentaru spends an

SHETHOSH AND ALEPH RECURSION KEY

It's unlikely to come up during the adventure, but Uentaru has a secret base that no one knows about (though the Dustman suspects): a pocket-dimension-sized recursion she calls Shethosh.

In her base, Uentaru keeps extra supplies, a few cyphers, and her most prized possession: an Aleph component recursion key. This partly melted metallic object strung on a pendant is a recursion key for the subterranean chamber where the Aleph component resides under Earth's mantle. The PCs are unlikely to find Shethosh unless desperation from a malfunctioning REV (described in the final chapter) forces them to come up with other options for journeying deep into the Earth. The translation gate for Shethosh is hidden on Earth in the form of a rolled-up poster, which is in the possession of Obol Demer, one of the spiral dust dealers that Uentaru helped set up. Obol has no idea of the poster's significance or provenance, and he keeps it in a separate storage unit from his home.

Recursion key, page 130

Obol Demer, page 34

GM Intrusion: *When the PC is hit by a blast from the starshine lance, she catches fire and burns for an additional 5 points of ambient damage each round on her turn until someone spends a turn smothering the flames.*

GM Intrusion: *The Dustman fixes his burning sapphire gaze on a PC within long range. If the character fails a difficulty 5 Intellect defense roll, she is stunned into inactivity for one round by this psychic attack.*

Entropic seed, page 219

Experience Point Awards: *The PCs gain 1 XP each for rescuing Jonathan Ballard and 1 XP each for rescuing Dram-shara. Turning on Uentaru and sending her packing is worth 2 XP for each PC, as is either allying with or defeating the Dustman and recovering the entropic seed. These awards are in addition to any XP earned for recovering artifacts or by other means.*

action tending to her wounds, she regains 6 points of health (thanks to her golden armor).

If Uentaru spends an action reconfiguring her golden armor, she can make it impervious to heat, cold, or another extreme environment (only one type at a time) for up to an hour. Doing so reduces the Armor value to 1 during that time.

Interaction: One of the functions of Uentaru's armor is to serve as a universal translator, allowing her to converse with most aliens she meets. She is driven and might seem honorable up to a point, but her goals are more important than anything else, including any promises she might have made.

Loot: Uentaru carries a couple of cyphers, plus her golden armor and starshine lance, both of which are keyed only to her—anyone else would find the items difficult to use.

Modifications: All tasks related to stealth as level 8.

Combat: When the Dustman unleashes his shadowy aura, it acts like an immaterial digestive enzyme. This means that when he produces a greatsword apparently fashioned of shadow, its attack inflicts 6 points of damage from the impact and 4 points of damage from the digestive process. Moreover, anyone within immediate range of the Dustman when he attacks takes 1 point of damage each round from the enzymatic digestion. (Wounds the Dustman inflicts are stained blue because the victim's flesh has partly petrified. Someone killed by the Dustman completely petrifies, becoming a chalky blue statue—solid spiral dust.)

While within Nakarand or in immediate range of someone experiencing the effects of spiral dust, the Dustman regenerates 2

> *If the Dustman is killed, Nakarand retreats into the Strange, breaking through whatever barriers lie between. There Nakarand hides away until a new avatar forms, one that has the characteristics of creatures from the nearest prime world.*

THE DUSTMAN, AVATAR OF NAKARAND   6 (18)

The Dustman is the avatar of Nakarand, an alien creature native to the Strange. He serves as Nakarand's mind, hands, and will.

Sentient creatures usually see the Dustman right before or after they take the drug known as spiral dust. He has been described as "a malign sandman" who steals away through dream those who overindulge in his dust—which is true. Nakarand and, by extension, the Dustman feed on the flesh and minds of living creatures that become addicted to spiral dust, which ultimately leads victims to the entity's expandable stomach. If Nakarand is fed, so too is the Dustman.

Motive: Feed and defend Nakarand

Environment (the Strange | Any): The Dustman can appear in any recursion and is sometimes seen haunting the dreams of spiral dust users.

Health: 22

Damage Inflicted: 10 points

Armor: 2

Movement: Short

points of health each round.

Interaction: The Dustman seeks to hook new victims on spiral dust.

Loot: The Dustman carries 1d6 random cyphers, which he distributes to the PCs if they ally with him. He also carries an entropic seed, which he intends for the PCs to use to deactivate the Aleph component "from inside." Finally, he has a bag made of shadow that contains a few pounds of spiral dust.

By the end of this part of the adventure, the PCs might or might not have defeated Uentaru or the Dustman, but they have learned Uentaru's real plan and potentially gained an entropic seed. If they wish to stop her plan, the seed is a good start, but it must be used inside the Aleph component to have a chance of success (see "Using the Entropic Seed or Nuke" on page 88). The PCs might recall Hertzfeld talking about a vehicle he was working on that could be just what they need, as described in the next chapter.

JOURNEY TO THE CENTER OF THE EARTH

This part of the adventure is the finale of The Dark Spiral *and is appropriate for PCs who have learned about the Aleph component and the real reason that Uentaru secretly helped the Dustman increase the distribution of spiral dust. As a stand-alone scenario, "Journey to the Center of the Earth" offers the characters a chance to enjoy a scenario quite different from most others they'll encounter while playing* The Strange—*not to mention save the Earth and its recursions from destruction.*

BACKGROUND

A native of the Chaosphere (the Dustman, avatar of Nakarand) and an alien from the universe of normal matter who has lived in the Strange for thousands of years (Uentaru) conspired to dramatically increase the use of the drug spiral dust on Earth and its recursions. One spiral dust quality is to temporarily wake the user's mind to a state much like being quickened. Uentaru leveraged that quality to activate an ancient alien device buried deep under the Earth's crust, the Aleph component, which was embedded during the late heavy bombardment of the planet billions of years ago. She wants to use the Aleph component to recreate her own long-demolished alien world of Mycaeum.

SYNOPSIS

The PCs have to find a way to physically journey into the Earth. (Hertzfeld, the Estate's research chief, has a method.) Obviously, the trip offers its own challenges. If all goes well, they arrive in the subterranean bubble under the Earth that contains the Aleph component. Surviving the environment, defeating the horrifying guardian that Uentaru left behind, and possibly having to choose between their own lives and the continued existence of planet Earth will push the PCs to their limit, and perhaps beyond.

GETTING THE PCs INVOLVED

The most straightforward way to bring the PCs into the adventure is by having them learn about Uentaru's real plan, as revealed at the end of "Whole Body Grafts." If that doesn't work out, try the following option.

Non-Estate PCs: A quickened research scientist—which could be Hertzfeld of the Estate, a scientist working for the Office of

---

> ### ENTROPIC SEED ON EARTH
> If the PCs have the entropic seed provided by the Dustman, on Earth it takes the form of a rounded black briefcase. Inside is a liquid crystal interface where directions are input by voice command.

Strategic Recursion, or a researcher in Ruk—has noticed alarming patterns of data from various sources. The scientist hypothesizes that some kind of enormous, high-energy object deep beneath Earth's mantle has become perturbed. If current trends continue, Earth will eventually be rent asunder. The PCs are recruited to investigate the anomaly using an experimental craft referred to as a recursion engine vehicle or, as it's nicknamed, the REV.

MODIFYING FOR DIFFERENT TIERS

If the PCs are second-tier characters or lower, decrease the level of the inkling snatcher and extereon by 2. See Modifying a Creature's Level for additional guidance.

PREPARING TO SAVE THE WORLD

If the PCs return to the Estate (or another allied organization) with news of potential disaster hiding beneath the Earth, they are taken seriously. It's soon discovered that not much time remains, and the PCs are given every resource the organization can manage on such short notice.

TESTS CONFIRM THE END IS NIGH

The PCs are pulled into a small conference room. Besides the characters, the room holds all the senior staff of the Estate, including

Entropic seed, page 219

Modifying a Creature's Level, page 16

Estate roster, page 149

the enigmatic Fixer, who only observes. The floor is given to Hertzfeld, who begins a presentation slide show, complete with several data graphs.

• "Your warning was priceless. You're right; I've confirmed that the Earth has about five days before it's destroyed."

• "This data was collected from many sources around the world: seismographs, university gravimeters, the Super-Kamioka Neutrino Detection Experiment, radio and high-energy particle detectors, and even a couple of my own experimental dark energy flux detectors."

• "The data was there all along, but no one was making correlations. After we started looking, we discovered several trends that began to tick up a few years ago, but recently show a likelihood of spiking asymptotically!" (Hertzfeld presents a quick slide show of simple charts that begin as shallow trends but end with scary-looking slopes heading toward a spike. The spikes are all labeled with dates that average between three and seven days in the future.)

• "Even without your information regarding this 'Aleph component,' this data shows that some sort of destabilizing event is underway approximately 1,800 miles beneath the Earth's surface. If it's not stopped, not only will Earth suffer untold devastation from earthquakes and volcanoes, but it will be rent entirely asunder."

• "So how do we stop an alien device billions of years old from reactivating?" (If they haven't mentioned it already, the PCs can chime in here about how they have something called an entropic seed which, if brought into proximity with the Aleph component and used correctly, might do the trick.)

• "As it happens, an unrelated project of mine is a vehicle that might be able to reach the device under the mantle... though I've never had a completely successful test of it. I call it the recursion engine vehicle, or REV for short." (Hertzfeld flashes a slide of the vehicle in question, perhaps the very one he might have showed the PCs in "Estate Home Base.")

ADDITIONAL DATA AND PREPARATION

Hertzfeld's combined data streams reveal that an energetic object more than 100 miles (161 km) in diameter lies about 1,800 miles (2,900 km) below the surface of the Earth, right around the area where the thick, rocky mantle

gives way to the Earth's outer core. Hertzfeld points this out on a schematic of the Earth's interior.

Earth Salvation Team: The Estate staff determines that the PCs are the quickened agents who will take on the task of switching off the Aleph component, given their previous involvement. If they plan to use Hertzfeld's REV, he'll go along to help pilot the craft.

Destination: Crunching all the data even more finely, Hertzfeld determines that an open space nearly 20 miles (32 km) in diameter lies in a zone contiguous with the Aleph component. He theorizes that that's where the PCs have the greatest chance of succeeding in their intervention. Knowing where to go, he says, is half the problem. Having a way to get there is most of the rest of the solution, except for "a few additional considerations."

Protection: A destination so close to the core suggests that travelers will face dangerously high temperatures—several thousand degrees, in fact. While the REV cab should be able to maintain livable temperatures, once the PCs reach their destination, they might have to leave the cab. The Estate has two solutions.

Sun Suits: The PCs and Hertzfeld are each issued thin silvery suits with strange writing; Katherine Manners says the suits were retrieved from a burned-out recursion operating under the laws of Standard Physics that tried (and failed) to restart an analogue of their sun. The so-called sun suits will protect PCs against regular heat and should provide up to an hour's protection (but no more) even in the face of 6,000-degree Fahrenheit temperatures.

Heat Stop Cypher: A heat stop will give one PC a full hour of complete protection against heat. Unfortunately, the Estate has only one device to offer.

Other Cyphers: The Estate relaxes its policy of restricting free cyphers given to operatives during early missions and provides the characters with enough cyphers to bring them to their cypher limit. The devices offered are limited to the following selection: curative (x3), meditation aid (x4), analeptic (x1), nutrition and hydration (x2), phase wall (x1), recursion anchor (x1), reflex enhancer (x1), and Strange apotheosis (x1).

Final Resort: If the PCs' entropic seed doesn't work (or if they lost it or never obtained it), Lawrence Keaton introduces Colonel Angela Whitesides from OSR. She

---

Sun Suit: provides 5 Armor against direct damage from heat or fire; protects wearer from extreme constant heat for one hour before being compromised

Colonel Angela Whitesides: level 5, level 6 in all tasks related to strategy and tactics

gives the PCs a tactical nuke small enough to fit in a suitcase. She says that once it's activated, detonation time is ten minutes, which is cutting things fine whether the PCs retreat via the REV or through their own ability to translate.

THE JOURNEY BEGINS

Once the PCs are certain they've made all possible arrangements given the short preparation time, they begin the trek into the Earth. If they use Hertzfeld's REV, refer to the following section. If they devise some other method of travel, you still might be able to use one or more of the suggested Encounters Along the Descent.

TRAVELING IN THE RECURSION ENGINE VEHICLE

The REV is on the bottommost research level under the Recursion Lab on the Estate campus. Hertzfeld explains that given the REV's top movement speed of 80 miles (129 km) per hour, the journey to the Aleph component will take about 24 hours of continuous travel, assuming the unforeseen problems certain to crop up don't sap too much time.

REV Stats: level 6; health 18; Armor 4; two long-range plasma attacks that each inflict 7 points of damage if fired by pilot and copilot. When phasing, the REV has a top speed of 80 miles per hour in any direction.

REV Cab: The cab of the REV is large enough to hold up to six people comfortably, or eight with some crowding. Two seats are designated for the pilots, and the craft can be operated from either seat by manipulating the facing control panel. The other four seats are for passengers.

The REV also contains a bathroom quite similar to the one used by astronauts on the International Space Station; it's functional but hardly glamorous.

Life Support and Airlock: When the REV is in operation, it continually recirculates air between the cab and a pocket recursion that makes up the engine. The cab is accessible via an airlock; leaving the protective recursive field of the vehicle through the airlock puts the debarking passenger at the mercy of whatever conditions are like outside (presumably, incredible heat and possibly high pressure). Those inside remain within a phased bubble of protective reality.

Piloting the REV: Hertzfeld says a PC who

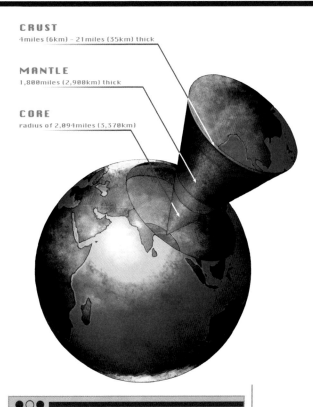

CRUST
4 miles (6km) – 21 miles (35km) thick

MANTLE
1,800 miles (2,900km) thick

CORE
radius of 2,894 miles (3,570km)

● ○ ○ ▬▬▬▬▬▬▬▬▬

HEAT STOP

Level: 1d6 + 3
Earth: Smartphone app
Ardeyn: Scroll inscribed with a spell
Ruk: Spine
Effect: When the device is activated, the user and all her possessions become immune to damage from heat or fire for one hour.

▬▬▬▬▬▬▬▬▬ ● ○ ○

---

is better at driving than him needs to take the job of primary pilot, but he's happy to be the copilot (thus serving as an asset to driving tasks). The REV uses the standard rules for vehicular movement, except the base difficulty for Speed-based tasks to drive the REV is 1 (not routine). On the other hand, an active copilot reduces the task to routine again. Failure results are based on the situation, but at minimum they usually mean that the REV loses about an hour in its race toward the Aleph component.

Sensors are crude while the REV is phasing through solid material, akin to submarine sonar. They can pick up very large density differentials, but not reliably. Other sensors, added by Hertzfeld, show the location and distance to the Aleph component. Transparent windows allow pilots to view the surroundings when the REV is not phasing.

Ⓢ

*Vehicular movement,
page 119*

What's That Big Red Button? As a last, desperate way to stop the cab from being destroyed, Hertzfeld explains that pressing the Big Red Button detonates explosive charges designed to jettison the recursion engine field. Doing so (he explains) will either kill everyone in a blast of light and heat as the REV is destroyed, or slingshot the cab into a random recursion in the Shoals of Earth. In the latter case, it would be akin to a translation failure (a particularly bad roll on the translation failure table, such as 86-90), except that instead of translating, the cab and passengers might end up in an unexpected location as if they were punted through an inapposite gate. But, says Hertzfeld, it's hard to be certain.

ENCOUNTERS ALONG THE DESCENT

The REV could encounter a few challenges as it descends toward its target. Use some, all, or none of these as seems prudent. If the PCs are using some other method to descend, consider adapting these encounters to that method.

UENTARU STRIKES BACK

During Intermission 2, Uentaru gave the PCs a communicator artifact. If they still have it, the communicator's special effect grants it the status of a recursion key endpoint, allowing Uentaru's servitors to find and attack the characters. And one does just that when the PCs are a few hours into their descent within the tiny cab of the REV, not long after Hertzfeld takes a break to lie down and rest.

Is That Smoke? Black vapor begins to issue from the communicator, though the source is probably not immediately apparent and might be diagnosed as a malfunction in the REV. After three rounds, an inkling snatcher resolves, whispers, "Uentaru said I could have whatever I found at the other end," and attacks.

The inkling snatcher preferentially attacks the REV pilots. (Remember to modify the inkling's level if the PCs' tier is too low or too high.)

GM Intrusion: A successful attack against a PC pilot causes the REV to spin out of control. In the short term, the Coriolis effect caused by the spinning affects the PCs' attacks on the inkling: each time a character misses the creature, the attack is made against the interior of the REV instead. The vehicle's Armor doesn't count against such attacks.

Repercussions: At minimum, this encounter means that the REV loses valuable time on the way to its destination. The vehicle might also sustain damage, in addition to any lasting damage inflicted on characters.

SEISMO-STRANGE ANOMALY

Just before the PCs arrive at their destination (when they're 1,700 miles or 2,736 km into the planet), Hertzfeld excitedly tells them to look at the sensors.

• "Something's going on. The energy signature of the Aleph component just spiked and then dropped off again. But some sort of secondary wave is spreading out from the event, both down into the core and up into the mantle. In about ten seconds, it's going to sweep across us. Get ready!"

• "If it's strictly seismological, we should weather it just fine. But if there's a dark energy component, we may be in for—"

Anomalous Wave: The wave hits the REV like a hammer hitting an anvil. Sparks burst from every monitor, the noise is shattering, red lights and alarms go off, and the vehicle enters into another spin. In addition, quickened PCs discover that special abilities granted by their type have become somewhat "fuzzed."

REV Spin: Saving the REV requires a series of tasks. The pilot or pilots must pull the vehicle out of its spin by making two successful difficulty 5 Intellect-based rolls before failing three rolls.

If three failures are rolled before two successes, add another malfunction to the two described below, and start the piloting attempts over again. Not attempting to gain control of the spin on a given round counts as one failure.

REV Malfunctions: While the pilots attempt to pull the REV out of its spin, the other PCs need to attend to other system malfunctions. Mechanics must make two (or more, if the pilots fail in their attempts, as described above) successful difficulty 5 Intellect-based rolls to repair the electronics and mechanical systems before failing three attempts. Not attempting to fix the REV on a given round counts as one failure.

If three failures are rolled before the required successes, the PCs probably need to press the Big Red Button to save themselves because the REV begins to crumble around them. Pushing the button takes courage, since the PCs probably expect that it will end

Translation failure table, page 128

Communicator, page 29

Inkling snatcher, page 273

their mission. But not to worry: thanks to the Aleph component's distortion of the dark energy network less than 100 miles (161 km) away, instead of being kicked into a random recursion, the dead REV cab appears 50 feet (15 m) above the ground in the Aleph vault and drops the PCs at the foot of the component.

Anomalous Type Ability "Fuzzing": If the PCs attempt to use their type abilities, they might have unusual results. A roll of 1 or 2 causes a GM intrusion. On the other hand, if a PC rolls a natural 17, 18, 19, or 20, the positive effect is doubled.

Dustman: If the Dustman joined the PCs as an ally, the anomalous wave instantly exiles him to the Chaosphere and prevents him from returning to the vicinity of the Aleph component. His disappearance is preceded by his verbal exclamation, "That's strange…" followed by an audible "pop."

ALEPH VAULT

read aloud

The mantle opens into a mammoth, miles-wide cyst. The area is lit by rivulets of white-hot magma along the far walls and an atmosphere so hot it's luminous, yet somehow not burning. Bathed in that unforgiving light is a structure that pulls at the human brain like a blind spot revealed. It protrudes from the floor, only partly unearthed, but utterly alien in its geometry.

Conditions in the Vault: Temperatures are not as hot as they should be (nor pressure as crushing), but the temperature is still about 1,000 degrees Fahrenheit (538 C). Once the PCs leave the protection of the REV, they'll have only about an hour to accomplish their purpose if they use the sun suits provided by the Estate. Like the suits, other measures that protect the PCs from heat also protect them from breathing in the superheated air.

Anomalous Type Ability "Fuzzing": The ability fuzzing previously described continues to affect the PCs while they remain in the vault or the Aleph component. The Dustman likewise remains fenced out of the vicinity.

ALEPH COMPONENT

The Aleph component is oppressively large. Luckily for the PCs, study of the exterior reveals a break in the side of the sloping wall of alien technology, where someone (Uentaru) has forced an entry.

Show 'Em: Aleph Component, Image L, page 96

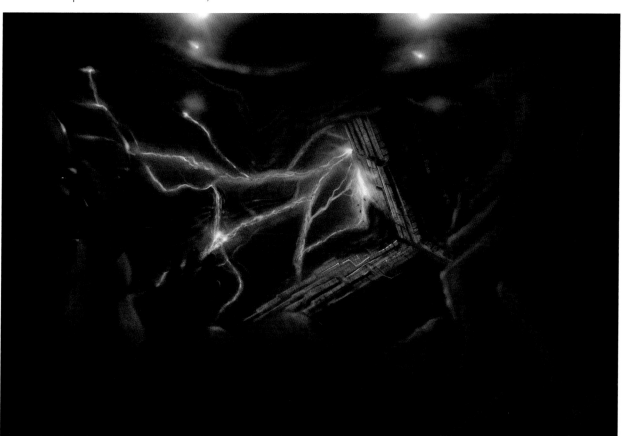

1. GOLDEN ENTRANCE

A break in the surface of the component is coated in what looks like melted gold, though it's actually nanotechnology deployed by Uentaru to keep the breach open (otherwise, the Aleph heals itself). The Aleph is composed of a synthetic material advanced beyond the capability of human science to catalogue.

2. ALEPH INTERIOR

read aloud

The interior space of the Aleph component looks similar to the exterior, composed of thousands of flat ivory- and amber-colored surfaces in faceted series that form irregular floors, walls, and ceilings. Though the chamber before you is discrete, there is a sense that at any moment the entire cavity might fold out or in, reconfiguring itself into some new mazelike space.

Group GM intrusion, page 341

If the PCs press anywhere along the walls, they trigger minor reconfigurations in wall shape and height. Every step they take does the same on the floor, like ripples on a pool's surface. But while current conditions hold in area 3, nothing more serious occurs.

White Glow: It's dark inside the Aleph except for a golden glow leaking from the exit that leads toward area 3.

3. CONTROL INTERFACE

The Chaos Templars secretly induced the extereons' home sun to go nova and then swooped in to "save" a subsection of the race.

read aloud

A horrifying creature stands in this chamber, its odd limbs flexing and quivering as if it waits for some sign. Behind it, the far wall of the chamber is damaged. A massive glob of golden substance surrounds an irregular cavity, like blood around a bullet wound. Revealed in the cavity is a flickering tube of white energy that

passes from one end of the hole to the other.

Uentaru learned about the Aleph component in this chamber, figuring out how to wake it and how to program it to recreate her own lost planet of Mycaeum in the aftermath of Earth's destruction. By the time the PCs arrive, there is no time to reprogram the alien technology, even if they understood the workings of the golden nanotech. They have two options: use the entropic seed, or use the tactical nuke supplied by OSR.

Extereon: Before the PCs can make a decision, they're attacked by the extereon, the guardian that Uentaru left in the control interface room.

What About Uentaru? If the PCs killed her, she's gone. If they merely defeated her (or if she got away), she might choose this moment to show up and join the fray in a last-ditch attempt to defeat the PCs; treat it as a group GM intrusion.

EXTEREON 8 (24)

Extereons are native to the universe of normal matter, but from a world far distant from Earth in time and space. Eyelike protuberances provide them with a 360-degree view of their surroundings, and multiple prehensile limbs allow them to manipulate what they spy around them with machinelike precision. Extereons once thrived in an environment of extreme temperature with a sulfuric acid atmosphere. Right before their sun went nova, a group of Chaos Templars saved several extereons by transferring them to a haven in the Strange. For this good deed, the surviving extereons and their descendants remain extraordinarily grateful.

An extereon's prehensile limbs seep acid, and its eyes have the psychic power to strike terror in prey.

GM Intrusion: When a PC is damaged in combat, her sun suit is torn! She must use one hand to hold the rent closed (which means the difficulty of all physical tasks she attempts is increased by one step) or suffer 1 point of ambient heat damage each round.

USING THE ENTROPIC SEED OR NUKE

To successfully use the entropic seed, the PCs must activate it in front of the open control interface (where the line of white energy is revealed in the cavity of room 3). Activating the seed is as simple as "making a wish" as part of a difficulty 1 Intellect-based task. Unless the PC fumbles the roll or "wishes" for something completely unrelated to saving Earth, turning the Aleph off, returning it to its former status, and so on, the component goes back to sleep and becomes immune to the greater number of quickened people around Earth.

If the PCs instead activate the nuke, it has a similar effect, but only by blowing a massive hole (a few miles in diameter) in the Aleph, which takes several months for the component to heal. While it does so, all creatures with quickened abilities find that the difficulty of actions granted by those abilities is modified by two steps to their detriment. However, the PCs' more immediate concern is getting away from the blast radius within ten minutes (tops), at which point the nuke detonates.

Motive: Survival, pay debt to Chaos Templars through service

Environment (the Strange | Standard Physics): Anywhere Chaos Templars roam

Health: 24

Damage Inflicted: 6 points

Movement: Immediate

Modifications: Perception as level 9; speed defense as level 5 due to size and nature.

Combat: The creature attacks by simply touching its foes and can make three melee touch attacks as one action. Standard material objects that would strike an extereon (even bullets and other high-velocity attacks) are mostly eaten away by acid, so the creature takes only one-quarter the damage (round down) from any physical attack made against it. Objects whose level is less than the extereon's level are destroyed if they touch the creature, after dealing whatever damage they deal. However, raw energy, such as from a ray emitter or an explosion, affects an extereon normally. (Special objects, such as artifacts, that strike the extereon are not destroyed if the PC succeeds on a difficulty 5 Might defense roll.)

When an extereon attacks, it fixes its terrifying eyes on all creatures within immediate range. Opponents in range must make an Intellect defense roll against unreasoning (psychically induced) fear. On a failed roll, the victim freezes in terror for one round. This psychic attack is not an action for the extereon. For frozen prey, the difficulty to dodge the extereon's melee attacks is increased by three steps, and a successful attack inflicts 2 additional points of damage.

Interaction: Those with telepathic abilities (or a device that provides the same) might be able to establish a dialogue with one of these acidic horrors. If so, the PC would find it difficult to negotiate with an extereon if it involves contravening the wishes of a Chaos Templar.

Use: The PCs must find a specific artifact, but it's in the keeping of Chaos Templars in a facility in the Strange, guarded by extereons.

4. ALEPH INTERIOR

A PC could become utterly lost in the mazelike, lightless interior of the massive Aleph component, which has a penchant for reorganizing its paths without seeming purpose or reason. A brilliant white light shows the way to room 3, but everyplace else is dark.

PCs who persist on exploring the Aleph might find particularly weird locations. However, each time they progress to a new area (requiring about 2d6 minutes of travel), the route they used to get there reshuffles behind them, requiring a difficulty 3 Intellect-based check to find the path back.

Each additional time the PCs press deeper, the return route reshuffles more completely, increasing the difficulty of the return trip by one step. A failed attempt to find the way back means the PCs must rely on the rules for retrying a task or, if they've exhausted that option, translating to another recursion.

PCs who risk exploring the component

GM Intrusion: *The PC's weapon is slapped by an acidic tentacle. If the PC fails a difficulty 5 Speed defense roll, her weapon is destroyed. If the weapon is an artifact, the difficulty of the defense roll is decreased by two steps.*

Retrying a task, page 102

might find areas and objects that delight and terrify, including the following.

• The characters walk through an arch that disassembles and reassembles them in a flash. Everything seems the same afterward, except for newly acquired dark splotches on their skin that resemble faces.

• They discover a level 6 artifact (part of a larger indecipherable mechanism) that can be used to fire a beam of energy within short range. The artifact has two settings. One

setting causes the beam to act as propulsion, which rockets the artifact away unless the user can hold onto it with a Might-based task. The other setting fires a reactionless beam that can be used as a long-range plasma attack that inflicts 6 points of damage plus 1 additional point for each point the user spends from his Intellect Pool (as if using a special ability). Depletion: 1–2 in 1d20.

• They find a crystal vial filled with ten amber chewable tablets that act like level 5 age taker cyphers (without counting against a user's cypher limit).

• A second instance of a character is formed as an NPC under the control of the GM. The NPC has the PC's memories and equipment and many of her abilities, but the inhabiting intelligence is alien and potentially malign.

Age taker, page 313

ENDING THE ADVENTURE

If the PCs fail to shut down the Aleph component, things look grim for the Earth, but it doesn't have to be the end. As it turns out, OSR's Colonel Angela Whitesides recruited a second backup team with a bigger nuke (but no entropic seed). Just when things seem darkest, the second team could show up to revive defeated PCs, or the players could step into the shoes of the second team to complete the task where their original characters failed.

However, it's more likely that the PCs win the day, and some of them probably even survive. When these victors return to the surface, the Estate holds a ceremony in their honor (even if the PCs are not operatives of the Estate). In addition to goodwill, congratulatory speeches, and a wonderful party, each PC is given an artifact from Earth, Ruk, or Ardeyn, as chosen by the GM.

If the Dustman was killed (or dispersed during the anomalous wave), another avatar of Nakarand forms. Spiral dust might once again make its way to Earth, but without the aid of Whole Body Grafts and Uentaru, the number of addicts drops. If the Dustman survives, he retains a soft spot in his "heart" for the PCs, unless they come after him or Nakarand again.

If Uentaru survived, she licks her wounds and swears eternal vengeance against the PCs and the Estate. Eventually, she'll try something else, possibly involving the rest of the Chaos Templars and a planetovore lure, but that's far beyond the scope of this adventure.

This concludes *The Dark Spiral*. We hope you and your players found it exciting, challenging, and rewarding.

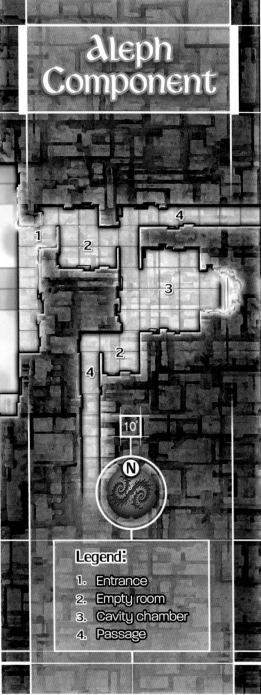

Aleph Component

Legend:
1. Entrance
2. Empty room
3. Cavity chamber
4. Passage

10'

N

A.

B.

C.

D.

E.

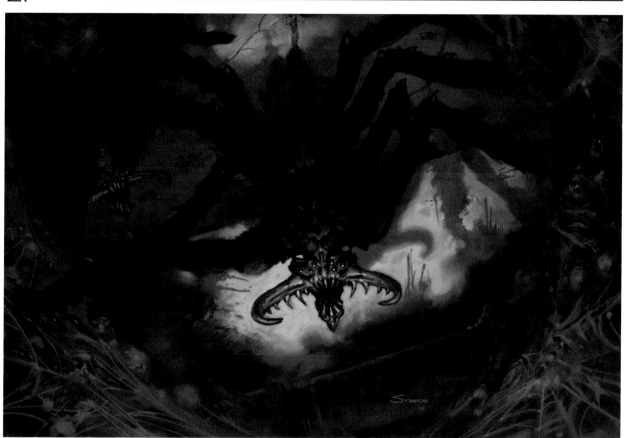

F.

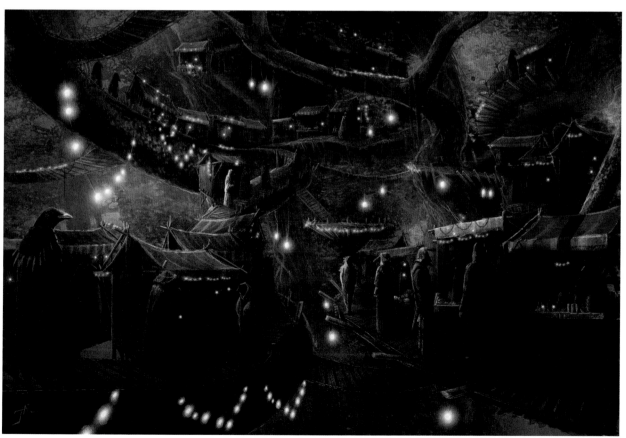

G.

H.

I.

J.

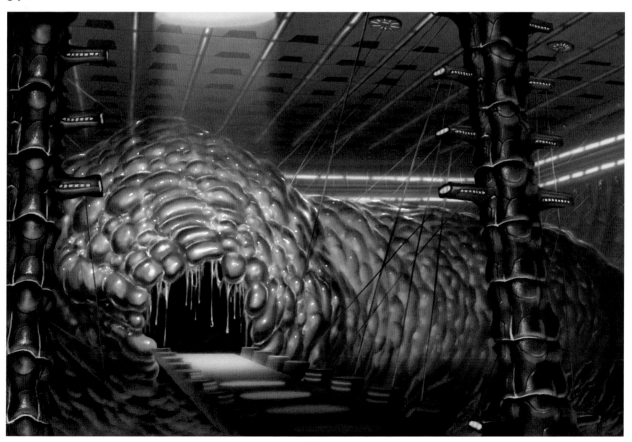

K.

L.

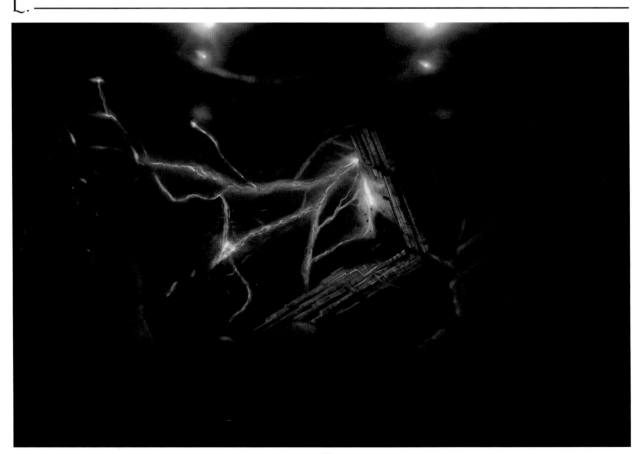